MW01246067

THE SCARLET THREAD
FINDING JESUS
THROUGH
OLD TESTAMENT PROPHECY

DAVID R. HOBSON

ISBN: 9798862022506
Independently Published

*To my family, who have stood
by me in these last days.
I love you all dearly.*

*To my precious Lord and Savior,
Jesus Christ, who I come to
"By the Way of the Cross"
and am looking forward
to meeting face-to-face.*

"I have nothing to claim but my guilt and my shame.
Hopelessly lost, I could not find my way.
Till His glorious light of love shone down on me.
His mercy washed all my sins away!
And what He did for me that day
Was a price I could not pay.
And by His grace, I too can forever say

I have come by the way of the cross.
I have come by the way of the cross.
It is nothing I have done.
It's the suffering of God's Son.
I have come by the way of the cross."

- By the Way of the Cross
The Ruppes

TABLE OF CONTENTS

PREFACE

Hearing of the five-hour sermon preached to his congregation by Texas pastor Dr. W.A. Criswell on New Year's Eve, 1961, I was fascinated. This lengthy sermon, called The Scarlet Thread Through the Bible, traced the message of redemption from Genesis to Revelation. This launched my personal survey of Old Testament prophecies specific to the Messiah, the Lord Jesus Christ. During many hours spent driving, I listened to numerous messages by Dr. David Jeremiah, Dr. J. Vernon McGee, Dr. Charles Stanley and others that greatly influenced my study and my personal relationship with Jesus.

My examination of Scripture was begun just to satisfy my own curiosity. After several months of study and discussions with my wife, Linda, she encouraged me to develop an outline that could be shared with my Sunday School class, family and friends. Having illegible handwriting and not being much of a typist, I started by making voice recordings of my findings. Linda later transcribed my recordings into a list of Scripture references, each with a sentence or two explaining my reason for including that particular prophecy.

As I delved deeper into the Bible, I came to realize that others might benefit from my study. Using my original outline, the very brief annotations were developed into paragraphs and sometimes pages, again via voice recordings. Linda diligently transcribed my ramblings, editing and making helpful suggestions along the way. Without her, this composition could never have been completed.

This is by no means an exhaustive study of Bible prophecy. It is my prayer that you will find the desire to study the Bible for yourself. I encourage you not to take my interpretations at face value; rather, compare them to God's Word by reading and studying on your own. Perhaps this book will be a helpful guide for you.

In writing this, I understand that many people spend most of their time in the New Testament. Of course, it is important to read and study the New Testament. However, I believe in order to understand that portion of Scripture, it is imperative to read and study the Old Testament – especially the prophecies, many of which have been fulfilled to the letter. Realizing that so many prophecies have been fulfilled should leave no doubt in mind that the remaining prophecies will be fulfilled exactly as they are written.

After working on this project for some years, life interfered and I abandoned the book idea. The many hours spent studying the Bible and prophecy had taught me so much about God's Word, I was satisfied to not see the book published. However, after being diagnosed with incurable cancer, even though I had not worked on it in a number of years, I began to feel the nudging of the Holy Spirit to complete this project. With the encouragement of my wife, I decided to finish this book before my life on this earth is finished.

My trust is in Jesus Christ, my Lord and Savior. I believe that He died on the Cross, shedding His precious blood for sinners like me. I believe He arose on the third day, and now sits at the right hand of God, and that He will come again just as His Word declares. The darkness of this world today sometimes may cause our beliefs to falter. It is my sincere hope that this book will bolster someone whose faith is weak. If it helps only one person, then this endeavor will have been worthwhile.

As this book nears completion, I am probably in my last six months of life. Chemotherapy affected me so badly I decided to cease and throw myself on the mercy of the Lord. I look forward to meeting my precious Savior face-to-face, as I go *"By the Way of the Cross. It is nothing I have done, but the suffering of God's Son."*
I thank the Father, Son and Holy Spirit.

In His Service,
Dave

CHAPTER 1: SEED OF THE WOMAN
Approximately 4000 BC

Genesis 3:15
> And I will put enmity
> Between you and the woman,
> And between your seed and her seed;
> He shall ªbruise you on the head,
> And you shall bruise him on the heel."

Our study begins at the beginning of the Bible, with the first foreshadowing of Christ. As the Biblical account unfolds, other events and statements regarding the Messiah, the Lord Jesus Christ, become more clear and more abundant. By the end of the Old Testament, a fairly complete picture of Christ has been drawn.

Throughout history, we find only one descendant of Eve who was born of woman without the involvement of a man. This verse is so important that it should be memorized by every Christian. It is the first prophecy in the Bible of the coming Messiah – the Savior – into the world. Notice that the Scripture says God "will put enmity Between you and the woman," not between you and mankind. Also notice it says "between your seed and her seed." This is the first foretelling of Christ being born to a virgin.

The most prominent thought in this verse is not that of the ultimate victory in the end, which will come. Rather, it reveals the fact of a continuing struggle between good and evil down through the ages. This struggle is exactly what we find described throughout the Scriptures. The Lord Jesus made the following statement in His day, concerning this struggle.

---

a. Genesis 3:15 or *crush*

John 8:44

> You are of *your* father the devil, and you want to do the desires of your father. He was a murderer from the beginning, and does not stand in the truth because there is no truth in him. Whenever he speaks [a]a lie, he speaks from his own *nature*, for he is a liar and the father of [b]lies.

In this passage the Lord Jesus made the distinction between the children of God and the children of Satan. An objective look at what is occurring in the world today provides an unequaled example of this struggle, taking place before our eyes. We have before us the facts: there is a conflict, there is a struggle, there are two seeds in the world, and there will be a final victory.

The long, continuous struggle is important to note. Each and every person must face temptation and must win this battle. Before Christ came into the world, victory was through obedience and faith. For example, Abraham's faith was counted as righteousness. Now, after Christ's first coming, we should identify – we must identify – ourselves with Christ, through faith.

---

a. John 8:44 lit *the lie;* b. lit *it*

CHAPTER 2: ABEL'S OFFERING
Approximately 4000 BC

Genesis 4:3-5
> So it came about [a]in the course of time that Cain brought an offering to the LORD of the fruit of the ground. 4 Abel, on his part also brought of the firstlings of his flock and of their fat portions. And the LORD had regard for Abel and for his offering; 5 but for Cain and for his offering He had no regard. So Cain became very angry and his countenance fell.

Translated from the Hebrew language, the "course of time" means the "end of the work week." In this case, it indicates the Sabbath day – the day God rested. Cain and Abel each brought an offering to God, to an appointed place, to worship, according to revelation (specific instruction) from God.

Hebrews 11:4
> By faith Abel offered to God a better sacrifice than Cain, through which he obtained the testimony that he was righteous, God testifying [b]about his gifts, and through [c]faith, though he is dead, he still speaks.

We see that "through faith" Abel brought his sacrifice to God. Apparently Cain, having also brought an offering to God, did not come by faith. He came on his own, and the offering he brought – not a blood sacrifice – denied that human nature is evil. God's instruction was to bring a blood sacrifice, a depiction of the Redeemer who later would come into the world. We must come to God on the basis of faith in a sacrifice; not by bringing the works of our own hands.

---

a. Genesis 4:3 Lit *at the end of days*
b. Hebrews 11:4 I.e. by receiving his gifts; c. Lit *it*

Cain's offering denied that man was separated from God (and had been since Adam and Eve were removed from the Garden of Eden). In today's world, liberalism denies this separation by promoting the universal fatherhood of God and the universal brotherhood of man. Things are not all right with us today; we are not born children of God. We have to be "born again" to be children of God. Man, by nature, is separated from God. Cain refused to recognize that separation. Multitudes refuse to do so today.

The righteousness of Cain was his own righteousness. The righteousness of Abel was faith in a sacrifice; a faith which down through the ages looked forward to Christ's ultimate sacrifice.

CHAPTER 3: THE CALL OF ABRAHAM
Approximately 2000 BC

Genesis 12:1-3

Now the Lord said to Abram,

> "[a]Go forth from your country,
> And from your relatives
> And from your father's house,
> To the land which I will show you;
> 2 And I will make you a great nation,
> And I will bless you,
> And make your name great;
> And so [b]you shall be a blessing;
> 3 And I will bless those who bless you,
> And the one who [c]curses you I will [d]curse.
> And in you all the families of the earth will
> be blessed."

Notice God's three-fold promise – a promise repeated several times in the Old Testament. The first part of the promise concerned the land. God said, 'I am going to show you a land, and I am going to give it to you.' The second part concerned the nation. "I will make you a great nation," and, "I will bless you, and make your name great." God also promised, "I will bless those who bless you," and, "the one who curses you I will curse." The third part was that God would make Abram a blessing. "And in you all the families of the earth will be blessed."

This brings up a question. Has God made good on His promise to Abram? God has certainly brought from him a great nation, which arguably has the longest tenure as a nation of any people on this earth.

---

a. Genesis 12:1 Lit *Go for yourself*
b. Genesis 12:2 Lit *be a blessing*
c. Genesis 12:3 Or reviles; d. Or *bind under a curse*

Galatians 3:8

> The Scripture, foreseeing that God [a]would justify the [b]Gentiles by faith, preached the gospel beforehand to Abraham, *saying*, "ALL THE NATIONS WILL BE BLESSED IN YOU."

Has Abraham (God changed Abram's name to Abraham in Genesis 17:5) been a blessing to all mankind? The answer is absolutely "Yes" – through the Lord Jesus Christ, he has been a blessing to the whole world. The entire Word of God has come to us through Abraham. God has fulfilled parts two and three of His promise, leaving only the first part to be accomplished.

God said, 'Abraham, I am going to give you that land.' Look what is happening in the Middle East today – for certain, tremendous turmoil. And the land Israel occupies today is only a small fraction of what God intends to give this nation.

So far, two-thirds of the promise has been fulfilled to the very letter. God said He would not let Israel occupy the land if they were disobedient. From the Bible, we know that Israel was disobedient and God removed them from that promised land. They remain away from Him today, and He continues to keep them from that land. God is doing exactly what He said He would do.

Eventually, God will return the people of Israel to the promised land. They will have more than just a toehold. Israel will own all the land east of the Euphrates river, north to the former Hittite nation, and south to the river of Egypt (a little river in the Arabian desert). Israel has never occupied all the land given them. At the zenith of their power they occupied 30,000 square miles, but God actually gave them 300,000 square miles. Israel has a long way to go.

---

a. Galatians 3:8 Lit *justifies;* b. Lit *nations*

Only on God's terms, and at God's appointed time, will they receive this promised reward.

Genesis 18:17-18
> The LORD said, "Shall I hide from Abraham what I am about to do, 18 since Abraham will surely become a great and [a]mighty nation, and in him all the nations of the earth will be blessed?

From this verse we learn of the tremendous influence that Abraham will have – in fact, is having even today – on multitudes of people.

Genesis 22:18
> In your [b]seed all the nations of the earth shall [c]be blessed, because you have obeyed My voice."

What seed is God referring to in this verse? Paul interprets the meaning.

Galatians 3:16
> Now the promises were spoken to Abraham and to his seed. He does not say, "And to seeds," as *referring* to many, but *rather* to one, "And to your seed," that is, Christ.

Thus we have the Bible's own interpretation of the seed. We assume that Abraham, Isaac, Jacob, and all of the other Old Testament leaders were great men in their day. Perhaps we feel that our modern day intellect is much better. I believe Abraham knew a great deal more about the coming of Christ and the Gospel than is generally recognized. Notice that the Lord Jesus said:

---

a. Genesis 18:18 Or *populous*
b. Genesis 22:18 Or descendants; c. Or *bless themselves*

John 8:56

> Your father Abraham rejoiced [a]to see My day, and he saw *it* and was glad."

This statement indicates that Abraham must have understood what was to take place, especially since the Savior had not yet come into the world, and would not appear for approximately 1,900 years.

---

a. John 8:56 Lit *in order that he might see*

CHAPTER 4: MELCHIZEDEK

Genesis 14:18-20
And Melchizedek king of Salem brought out bread and wine; now he was a priest of [a]God Most High.
19 He blessed him and said,

> "Blessed be Abram of [b]God Most High,
> [c]Possessor of heaven and earth;
> 20 And blessed be [d]God Most High,
> Who has delivered your enemies into your hand."

He gave him a tenth of all.

As we look at this passage, several questions come to mind. To begin with, where did this man Melchizedek come from? He just walked out on a page of Scripture with bread and wine, blessed Abram, and then walked off the page. Most of the important people in the Bible have a recorded lineage. This lack of ancestral detail is strange, because the Book of Genesis is the "Book of Families." It provides information about the beginnings and generations of these families. Each time someone important in the genealogical line in mentioned, his parents are also mentioned – 'he is the son of,' or 'these are the generations of.' Yet we do not find a record anywhere in Scripture of the generations of Melchizedek.

Melchizedek is mentioned in only three books of the Bible. In addition to this passage in Genesis, he is mentioned in Psalm 110:4, which is prophetic of Christ.

---

a. Genesis 14:18 Heb *El Elyon*
b. Genesis 14:19 Heb *El Elyon*; c. Or *Creator*
d. Genesis 14:20 Heb *El Elyon*

Psalm 110:4
> The LORD has sworn and will not [a]change
> His mind, "You are a priest forever
> According to the order of Melchizedek."

He is also mentioned several times in Hebrews. The writer of Hebrews makes it very clear that the reason there is no record of Melchizedek's father and mother, or beginning or ending of days, is because he portrayed the Christ which was to come. The priesthood of Christ, in its inception, is according to the order of Melchizedek – in that it has no beginning or end. Christ's priesthood follows the order of Aaron, but not His person. Our Lord had no beginning or ending of days.

Hebrews 7:21-22
> (for they indeed became priests without an oath, but He with an oath through the One who said to Him,
>
> > "THE LORD HAS SWORN
> > AND WILL NOT CHANGE HIS MIND,
> > 'YOU ARE A PRIEST FOREVER'");
>
> 22 so much the more also Jesus has become the guarantee of a better covenant.

As King, Christ is the son of Abraham. He is the son of David. This is clear from the Gospel of Matthew, but in the Gospel of John we read:

John 1:1
> In the beginning was the Word, and the Word was with God, and the Word was God.

Notice that Melchizedek brought bread and wine.

---

a. Psalm 110:4 Lit *be sorry*

1 Corinthians 11:26
> For as often as you eat this bread and drink the cup, you proclaim the Lord's death until He comes.

Melchizedek anticipated the death of Christ. Abram paid tithes to Melchizedek at the very beginning. How did he know about paying tithes? Evidently he had a revelation from God concerning this, as well as other matters of Hebrew tradition. We know from Scripture that Melchizedek was king of Salem (Jerusalem) and priest of the Most High God, El Elyon.

Hebrew tradition says that Melchizedek was Shem, the son of Noah and survivor of the flood – still alive – earth's oldest living man, and that he was a priest in the patriarchal age of the whole race. However, this may be incorrect, since Shem's lineage is provided. If so, this was a hint that God had already chosen (right after the flood) Jerusalem to be the scene of human redemption. Whoever he was, as both a priest and a king, Melchizedek was a picture and type of Christ.

Hebrews 5:7
> [a]In the days of His flesh, [b]He offered up both prayers and supplications with loud crying and tears to the One able to save Him [c]from death, and He [d]was heard because of His piety.

According to Psalm 110 and Hebrews 5:7 we do know that Melchizedek conferred a blessing on Abram, and Abram's response was to give him tithes, which was one-tenth of everything he possessed.

---

a. Hebrews 5:7 I.e. during Christ's earthly life; b. Lit *who having offered up*; c. Or *out of*, d. Lit *having been heard*

CHAPTER 5: ABRAHAM OFFERS ISAAC

Genesis 22:1-2
> Now it came about after these things, that God tested Abraham, and said to him, "Abraham!" And he said, "Here I am." 2 He said, "Take now your son, your only son, whom you love, Isaac, and go to the land of Moriah, and offer him there as a burnt offering on one of the mountains of which I will tell you."

Some translations say that God tempted Abraham, but tempt is not the best translation from the Hebrew. God does not tempt; He tests us to confirm our faith;

James 1:13
> Let no one say when he is tempted, "I am being tempted [a]by God"; for God cannot be tempted [b]by evil, and He Himself does not tempt anyone.

To prove our commitment;

Exodus 20:20
> Moses said to the people, "Do not be afraid; for God has come in order to test you, and in order that the fear of Him may [c]remain with you, so that you may not sin."

And to know our heart.

Deuteronomy 8:2
> You shall remember all the way which the LORD your God has led you in the wilderness these forty years, that He might humble you, testing you, to know what was in your heart, whether you would keep His commandments or not.

---

a. James 1:13 Lit *from*; b. Lit *of evil things*
c. Exodus 20:20 Lit *be before*

Satan, on the other hand, tempts us on a daily basis – with numerous attempts to draw us away from God; to keep us from following the will of God for our lives.

Genesis 22:6-9
> Abraham took the wood of the burnt offering and laid it on Isaac his son, and he took in his hand the fire and the knife. So the two of them walked on together. 7 Isaac spoke to Abraham his father and said, "My father!" And he said, "Here I am, my son." And he said, "Behold, the fire and the wood, but where is the lamb for the burnt offering?" 8 Abraham said, "God will [a]provide for Himself the lamb for the burnt offering, my son." So the two of them walked on together.
>
> 9 Then they came to the place of which God had told him; and Abraham built the altar there and arranged the wood, and bound his son Isaac and laid him on the altar, on top of the wood.

God promised that Isaac would be the Father of Nations.

Genesis 17:16
> I will bless her, and indeed I will give you a son by her. Then I will bless her, and she shall be *a mother of* nations; kings of peoples will [b]come from her."

Yet, God commanded that Isaac be killed before he had fathered any children. Abraham had faith that God would either provide an alternate sacrifice, or that He would bring Isaac back to life. He did not know *what* God would do, but he trusted Him completely. Abraham did not doubt it was the Voice of God who commanded him to do this deed. The idea originated

---

a. Genesis 22:8 Lit *see*
b. Genesis 17:16 Lit *be*

with God, not with Abraham. Abraham was willing to obey God's command, regardless of the outcome. This was the ultimate test of his faith.

Genesis 22:3-5

So Abraham rose early in the morning and saddled his donkey, and took two of his young men with him and Isaac his son; and he split wood for the burnt offering, and arose and went to the place of which God had told him. 4 On the third day Abraham raised his eyes and saw the place from a distance. 5 Abraham said to his young men, "Stay here with the donkey, and I and the lad will go over there; and we will worship and return to you."

The trip took three days – the length of time Christ was in the tomb. This is very much a sign of the future ultimate sacrifice – a father offering his only son – that is, the *only* Son of the Promise. Two thousand years later, at or very near this same site on Mount Moriah, God's own Son would be offered. Thus it was a foreshadowing, here at the birth of the Hebrew nation, of the grand event this nation was born to bring about.

Genesis 22:10-13

Abraham stretched out his hand and took the knife to slay his son. 11 But the angel of the LORD called to him from heaven and said, "Abraham, Abraham!" And he said, "Here I am." 12 He said, "Do not stretch out your hand against the lad, and do nothing to him; for now I know that you [a]fear God, since you have not withheld your son, your only son, from Me." 13 Then Abraham raised his eyes and looked, and behold, behind *him* a ram caught in the thicket by his horns; and Abraham went and took the ram and offered him up for a burnt offering in the place of his son.

---

a. Genesis 22:12 Or *reverence*; lit *are a fearer of God*

God called out to Abraham to stay his hand. Abraham passed the supreme test. Note that Abraham took the *ram* and offered it as the burnt offering. Remember in verse 8, Abraham said to Isaac, "God will provide for Himself the lamb for the burnt offering, my son." The *ram* was not that *lamb*. That event would take place some 2,000 years later.

Although the exact location of Abraham's attempt to sacrifice Isaac is not known, Genesis 22:2 says it was in the region of Moriah, and the writer of 2 Chronicles 3:1 indicates it was at or near that same site where Solomon later built the first temple.

2 Chronicles 3:1

Then Solomon began to build the house of the LORD in Jerusalem on Mount Moriah, where *the LORD* had appeared to his father David, at the place that David had prepared on the threshing floor of [a]Ornan the Jebusite.

Today this site is a Muslim Shrine. The Mosque of Omar was erected in 691 AD and stands on the Dome of the Rock; the peak of Mount Moriah.

---

a. 2 Chronicles 3:1 In 2 Sam 24:18, *Araunah*

CHAPTER 6: THE PROMISE REPEATED

Genesis 26:3-4

> Sojourn in this land and I will be with you and bless you, for to you and to your [a]descendants I will give all these lands, and I will establish the oath which I swore to your father Abraham. 4 I will multiply your [b]descendants as the stars of heaven, and will give your [c]descendants all these lands; and by your [d]descendants all the nations of the earth [e]shall be blessed;

God told Isaac not to leave the land and go to Egypt. God confirmed the covenant He made with Abraham, and repeated His three-fold promise. One, The Land: "to you and to your descendants I will give all these lands." Two, The Nation: "I will multiply your descendants as the stars of heaven." Three, The Blessing: "by your descendants all the nations of the earth shall be blessed." This same promise, made to Abraham, was reiterated here to Isaac. All the nations of the earth would be blessed through his line, down through the ages, to the Lord Jesus Christ.

Genesis 28:14

> Your [f]descendants will also be like the dust of the earth, and you will [g]spread out to the west and to the east and to the north and to the south; and in you and in your [h]descendants shall all the families of the earth be blessed.

In this passage of Scripture, God made exactly the same promise to Jacob that He had made to Abraham and Isaac. He confirmed and reaffirmed this to Jacob. A promise from God is a sure and certain thing.

---

a. Genesis 26:3 Lit *seed*
b. c. d. Genesis 26:4 Lit *seed*; e. Or *bless themselves*
f. Genesis 28:14 Lit *seed*; g. Lit *break through*; h. Lit *seed*

CHAPTER 7: HE TO WHOM
THE SCEPTER BELONGS

Genesis 49:10-11

> "The scepter shall not depart from Judah,
> Nor the ruler's staff from between his feet,
> [a]Until Shiloh comes,
> And to him *shall be* the obedience of the peoples.
> 11 "[b]He ties *his* foal to the vine,
> And his donkey's colt to the choice vine;
> He washes his garments in wine,
> And his robes in the blood of grapes.

Shiloh (Jesus) is the ruler. This is one of the most remarkable prophecies in the Word of God. We have previously seen that there would be a seed of the woman. That was the first prophecy, which we covered in Genesis 3:15. The seed of the woman, Messiah, will bruise the serpent's head. Messiah will be the victorious one. The seed was confirmed to Abraham, Isaac, Jacob, and then Judah. Out of Judah's line the Messiah would come. The word Shiloh means "rest and tranquility." When the Lord Jesus walked on the earth, He turned from those who rejected Him, and said to the populace.

Matthew 11:28

> "Come to Me, all [c]who are weary and heavy-laden, and I will give you rest.

Shiloh had come. Not only is Christ Shiloh, but He is also the One who will hold the scepter. The scepter of this universe will be held in His nail-pierced hands.

---

a. Genesis 49:10 Or *Until he comes to Shiloh*; or *Until he comes to whom it belongs*
b. Genesis 49:11 Lit *binding of*
c. Matthew 11:28 Or *who work to exhaustion*

Genesis 49:24

> But his bow remained [a]firm, And [b]his arms were agile,
> From the hands of the Mighty One of Jacob
> (From there is the Shepherd, the Stone of Israel),

Shiloh is also a Shepherd and a Stone. Later, in Numbers 24:17 we will find that a star is prophesied. This Star, the Messiah, is the seed promised to the woman and to the patriarchs. He is the Shiloh who brings rest, and He is the King who holds the scepter. He is the Shepherd who gave His life, and He is the Chief Shepherd who will return one day. He is the Stone that the builders rejected, who will now become Headstone of the corner – the Keystone which is the strength of the foundation. He is the Star – the Bright Morning Star for His Church.

This line passed from Adam to Seth after Abel was murdered; from Seth, through Noah to Shem, and Abraham, Isaac and Jacob, and now to Judah.

Genesis 49:11

> "[c]He ties *his* foal to the vine,
> And his donkey's colt to the choice vine;
> He washes his garments in wine,
> And his robes in the blood of grapes.

Who is referenced here? Christ rode into Jerusalem on a little donkey, and offered Himself as the Messiah, the King and the Savior. He washed His garments in wine – His own blood. When Christ returns His garments will be red, and the question is asked:

Isaiah 63:2

> Why is Your apparel red, And Your garments like the one who treads in the wine press?

---

a. Genesis 49:24 I.e. in an unyielding position; b. Lit *the arms of his hands*
c. Genesis 49:11 Lit *binding of*

This time the blood will not be His own, but that of His enemies. This passage predicts Christ's Second Coming, when He returns in judgment. This prophecy of Judah is one of the most significant in the Scriptures.

CHAPTER 8: THE INSTITUTION
OF THE PASSOVER

Exodus 12:1-2

Now the Lord said to Moses and Aaron in the land of [a]Egypt, 2 "This month shall be the beginning of months for you; it is to be the first month of the year to you.

As the Lord spoke to Moses and Aaron, He instituted what is considered to be the most important celebration of the Jewish Nation, "The Feast of the Passover" – a memorial to Israel's deliverance from Egypt.

Exodus 12:3-5

Speak to all the congregation of Israel, saying, 'On the tenth of this month they are each one to take a [b]lamb for themselves, according to their fathers' households, a [c]lamb for [d]each household. 4 Now if the household is too small for a [e]lamb, then he and his neighbor nearest to his house are to take one according to the [f]number of persons in them; according to [g]what each man should eat, you are to [h]divide the lamb. 5 Your [i]lamb shall be an unblemished male a year old; you may take it from the sheep or from the goats.

These lambs could not be just any lambs – they were required to be lambs without blemish.

---

a. Exodus 12:1 Lit *Egypt, saying*
b. Exodus 12:3 Or *kid*; c. Or *kid*; d. Lit *the*
e. Exodus 12:4 Or *kid*; f. Or *amount*; g. Lit *each man's eating*; h. Lit *compute for*
i. Exodus 12:5 Or *kid*

Exodus 12:6

[a]You shall keep it until the fourteenth day of the same month, then the whole assembly of the congregation of Israel is to kill it [b]at twilight.

Instructions were to slaughter the lamb in the evening, at twilight. Thousands of lambs were slain that evening. These many lambs were representative of another Lamb – one future Lamb, the Lord Jesus Christ – the Passover Lamb offered for us. This feast specifically describes the purpose of the coming of Lord Jesus to the world.

Exodus 12:7

Moreover, they shall take some of the blood and put it on the two doorposts and on the lintel [c]of the houses in which they eat it.

This verse gives specific instructions for the dispensation of the blood. The children of Israel were to put the blood of the lamb outside on their doorposts. Upon seeing the blood, the Death Angel would pass over (leave out) that house, thus saving the life of the first born in each individual family.

Exodus 12:8-10

They shall eat the flesh that *same* night, roasted with fire, and they shall eat it with unleavened bread [d]and bitter herbs. 9 Do not eat any of it raw or boiled at all with water, but rather roasted with fire, *both* its head and its legs along with its entrails. 10 And you shall not leave any of it over until morning, but whatever is left of it until morning, you shall burn with fire.

---

a. Exodus 12:6 Lit *It shall be to you for a guarding*; b. Lit *between the two evenings*

c. Exodus 12:7 Lit *upon*

d. Exodus 12:8 Lit *in addition to*

These are detailed instructions for the preparation, consumption, and disposal of the sacrifice. Specifically, this sacrifice could not be eaten raw, but must be roasted. When a person comes to Christ, he comes as a sinner. The sin in human lives must be roasted in the "fire of judgment." The sacrifice could not be boiled or soaked with water. This simply means that we must trust Christ, and Him alone. Unfortunately there are many today who trust in water, or a "watered-down" religion, for their salvation.

Exodus 12:11-12
Now you shall eat it in this manner: *with* your loins girded, your sandals on your feet, and your staff in your hand; and you shall eat it in haste—it is the LORD'S Passover. 12 For I will go through the land of Egypt on that night, and will strike down all the firstborn in the land of Egypt, both man and beast; and against all the gods of Egypt I will execute judgments—I am the LORD.

The Israelites were to be delivered out of Egypt and a life of slavery. God would deliver them as a people, and by individual families. God was readying Israel to leave Egypt – belt on, shoes on, staff in hand. He was also warning of the judgment to come, the execution of the firstborn of both man and beast.

When we come to Christ we should have our shoes and belt on, and be ready to get out of the world – to get out of "Egypt." This means we should no longer be involved in the sins of the world. A person cannot be converted and continue to live a sinful life. This does not mean that a person will not fall into sin occasionally; however, a true Christian will not make a habit of living in a pattern of sin.

Exodus 12:13

> The blood shall be a sign for you on the houses where you [a]live; and when I see the blood I will pass over you, and no plague will befall you [b]to destroy *you* when I strike the land of Egypt.

The Israelites were not saved because they were the seed of Abraham. Had the Egyptians known about the sacrificial lamb and blood on the doorposts, by following God's instructions they too would have been saved. God said, "When I see the blood I will pass over you."

No one was saved because of doing his best, or because he was honest, or because he was a good person. He was saved because of the *blood*. Israel was to have confidence and faith in the blood. They were not saved because they went through the ceremony of circumcision, or because they belonged to some synagogue. God said, "When I see the blood, I will pass over you."

The Death Angel was not taking a survey of the neighborhood. No one could open a window and tell the Death Angel how good they were, or how much charity work they had done. Anyone who stuck his neck out of a window that night would have found bad news. God said, "When I see the blood, I will pass over you." Nothing additional was needed.

By the same token, Christians today believe – by faith – that the shed blood of Christ, the Lamb, has saved them and *nothing else* is needed.

There are several references to a lamb in the New Testament.

---

a. Exodus 12:13 Lit *are*; b. Lit *for destruction*

John 1:29
The next day he *saw Jesus coming to him and *said, "Behold, the Lamb of God who takes away the sin of the world!

John 1:36
and he looked at Jesus as He walked, and *said, "Behold, the Lamb of God!"

1 Corinthians 5:7
Clean out the old leaven so that you may be a new lump, just as you are *in fact* unleavened. For Christ our Passover also has been sacrificed.

Revelation 5:6
And I saw [a]between the throne (with the four living creatures) and the elders a Lamb standing, as if slain, having seven horns and seven eyes, which are the seven Spirits of God, sent out into all the earth.

We see the blood of the lamb on the doorposts; the death of the firstborn in each family not protected by the blood; deliverance out of a hostile country; and, a celebration of the Feast of Passover throughout Israel's history. God painted a grand historical portrait of Christ – the Passover Lamb – and our deliverance by His blood from a hostile world, from the slavery of sin. As we review these scriptural passages we can see the relationship.

Many of the Hebrew people knew Moses as the deliverer. Although he was involved in the deliverance of Israel and was used greatly of God, the deliverance was not accomplished by Moses. Deliverance is first by *blood*, and that is the Passover – the death of the

---

a. Revelation 5:6 Lit *in the middle of the throne and of the four living creatures, and in the middle of the elders*

firstborn. In Exodus Chapters 13 and 14, crossing the Red Sea and the destruction of the Egyptian army was by *power*.

God delivered the people by *blood* and *power*. Our redemption today is by *blood* and *power*. The *blood* shed by Jesus on the Cross paid the penalty for our sins; the *power* of the Holy Spirit makes this ultimate sacrifice real and effectual in our hearts.

Zechariah 4:6
> Then he [a]said to me, "This is the word of the LORD to Zerubbabel saying, 'Not by might nor by power, but by My Spirit,' says the LORD of hosts.

Redemption is the work of the Lord Jesus on the Cross for our sins, and of the Holy Spirit within us.

---

a. Zechariah 4:6 Lit *said to me, saying*

CHAPTER 9: NO BONES TO BE BROKEN

There were very specific regulations for observing the Passover, and all of these regulations had to be followed exactly.

Exodus 12:46
It is to be eaten in a single house; you are not to bring forth any of the flesh outside of the house, nor are you to break any bone of it.

No bones were to be broken in the Passover lambs.

John 19:32-33
So the soldiers came, and broke the legs of the first man and of the other who was crucified with Him; 33 but coming to Jesus, when they saw that He was already dead, they did not break His legs.

It was common practice to break the legs of those being crucified, to speed death. Since Jesus had died by the time the soldiers broke the other crucified men's legs, there was no need to break His legs as well.

John 19:36
For these things came to pass to fulfill the Scripture, "NOT A BONE OF HIM SHALL BE [a]BROKEN."

---

a. John 19:36 Or *crushed or shattered*

CHAPTER 10: THE BRONZE SNAKE

Numbers 21:6-9

> The LORD sent fiery serpents among the people and they bit the people, so that many people of Israel died. 7 So the people came to Moses and said, "We have sinned, because we have spoken against the LORD and you; intercede with the LORD, that He may remove the serpents from us." And Moses interceded for the people. 8 Then the LORD said to Moses, "[a]Make a fiery *serpent*, and set it on a standard; and it shall come about, that everyone who is bitten, when he looks at it, he will live." 9 And Moses made a bronze serpent and set it on the standard; and it came about, that if a serpent bit any man, when he looked to the bronze serpent, he lived.

In this Scripture, Israel was to the point of dying. They knew they had sinned. They humbled themselves and admitted their sins. God had prepared an "out," or a healing for their sins. However, first He would force the people of Israel to look *by faith* upon this bronze serpent which He instructed Moses to construct.

Imagine that some of the people must have thought this was pure nonsense. These doubters required something more than receiving salvation by just gazing at a serpent made of brass. But the serpent could have remained there forever, and had the people not looked upon it as God instructed, they would never have been healed.

Looking forward almost 1,500 years, we see Jesus talking with Nicodemus that dark night.

---

a. Numbers 21:8 Lit *Make for yourself*

John 3:14-16

As Moses lifted up the serpent in the wilderness, even so must the Son of Man be lifted up; 15 so that whoever [a]believes will in Him have eternal life.

16 "For God so loved the world, that He gave His [b]only begotten Son, that whoever believes in Him shall not perish, but have eternal life.

Many of us today want to think of God as a church member, almost on our level. But we must begin our relationship with God as sinners.

Because of God's perfect nature, He cannot coexist with sin. We, with our imperfect nature, cannot remove ourselves from sin. On our own, there is no way for us to reach God – but He has provided a way. God loves us so much that He allowed His Son, the *Perfect Sacrifice*, to be offered up for us.

Because of His great love for us, God gave us a way to attain salvation. Scripture does not say God so loved the world that He saved the world. It says He "so loved the world, that He gave His only begotten Son."

Now, just as the people in Numbers looked upon the serpent, God says to us, '*look and live, look to Christ.*' He took our place on the Cross, and we must accept Him *by faith.* This is the only way for us to come to God.

---

a. John 3:15 Or *believes in Him will have eternal life*
b. John 3:16 Or *unique,* only one of His kind

CHAPTER 11: THE STAR

Numbers 24:17-19

> "I see him, but not now; I behold him, but not near;
> A star shall come forth from Jacob, A scepter shall rise
> from Israel, And shall crush through the [a]forehead of
> Moab, And [b]tear down all the sons of [c]Sheth.
> 18 "Edom shall be a possession, Seir, its enemies, also will
> be a possession, While Israel performs valiantly.
> 19 "One from Jacob shall have dominion,
> And will destroy the remnant from the city."

Have you ever wondered how the "wise men" knew
to look for a star? They were from the East – the Far
East. How could they associate a star with a King born
in Israel, and why would they make such a long journey
to a foreign land?

Nevertheless, about 1,500 years after this event was
foretold, we find coming out of the East (the land of
Balaam, son of Beor the Seer) a whole company of wise
men. Balaam was an outstanding and well known
prophet. His prophecy was accepted by the wise men.
They did not doubt where the star would lead them.

When the wise men arrived in Jerusalem, they
posed a question.

Matthew 2:2

> "Where is He who has been born King of the Jews?
> For we saw His star in the east and have come to
> worship Him."

Combining these Scriptures with the prophecy of
Daniel (who also prophesied in the East) we find the
approximate time the Messiah would come into the
world.

---

a. Numbers 24:7 Lit *corners*; b. Another reading is *the crown of the head of*;
c. I.e. tumult

~ 43 ~

The writings of the Old Testament were studied and memorized by the chief priests and teachers of The Law. When Herod called these men together to ask where the Christ was to be born, they very quickly answered "in Bethlehem in Judea." It is still remarkable that they did not believe what they studied so intently.

CHAPTER 12: A PROPHET LIKE MOSES — PROMISE OF THE COMING MESSIAH

Deuteronomy 18:15-19

> "The LORD your God will raise up for you a prophet like me from among you, from your [a]countrymen, you shall listen to him. 16 This is according to all that you asked of the LORD your God in Horeb on the day of the assembly, saying, 'Let me not hear again the voice of the LORD my God, let me not see this great fire anymore, or I will die.' 17 The LORD said to me, 'They have [b]spoken well. 18 I will raise up a prophet from among their [c]countrymen like you, and I will put My words in his mouth, and he shall speak to them all that I command him. 19 It shall come about that whoever will not listen to My words which he shall speak in My name, I Myself will require it of him.

The children of Israel were instructed to listen to God's prophets. First, that was the only way they had to study and learn what God had planned for them, and to know what He expected of them. Most of the people in that day, even if they had access to the Scriptures, could not read. Plus, it was very expensive to have the Word of God written on scrolls.

The second reason was to prepare the people to listen to the final Messenger – the final Prophet – the Christ. Some people ask why the Lord does not reveal Himself. In the person of the Lord Jesus Christ, He did reveal Himself. When Christ died on the Cross, His chapter in the book ended. He put the period at the end of the sentence, and He wrote finished. God has nothing more to say than what He said in Jesus Christ. We are to hear Him, pay attention to Him, and obey Him.

---

a. Deuteronomy 18:15 Lit *brothers*
b. Deuteronomy 18:17 Lit *done well what they have spoken*
c. Deuteronomy 18:18 Lit *brothers*

At the Transfiguration – the majestic and glorious appearance of Christ, witnessed by Peter, James and John, God said:

Matthew 17:5b
> ..."This is My beloved Son, with whom I am well-pleased; listen to Him!"

If we allow the Holy Spirit to guide us, He will give us insight to help us understand His Word. We have the Light and the Word; and, conversely, we have false teachers – many of them. We need to compare what we hear and read elsewhere against God's written Word, under the guidance of the Holy Spirit. He will give us discernment if we ask Him.

CHAPTER 13: KINSMAN-REDEEMER

Ruth is the story of a foreign girl who came from a country of paganism and idolatry. She was from Moab, from a people who were considered a heathen, outcast group. Ruth came to a knowledge of the Lord God of Israel and, as Boaz said, came to Him for refuge.

In just four short chapters, this book packs a mighty message. In fact, Ruth contains several messages. For one thing – probably the most important point – Ruth provides a genealogy that leads to the Lord Jesus Christ, and explains His being descended from the line of David. The book is very significant in this sense.

Without this book we could not connect the House of David with the tribe of Judah. It is an important link in the chain of Scripture which begins with Genesis and continues to the stable in Bethlehem – to the Cross, the Crown, and to the throne of David on which our Lord will eventually be seated.

Ruth is one of only two books in the Bible not named after a person of Jewish descent. Another extremely meaningful purpose of this book is that it presents an important step in the doctrine of redemption – *salvation* – which is possible only through a kinsman-redeemer. God could not redeem apart from a mediator. Since only God could redeem, it was necessary for Him to become that Person. The example of Boaz helps us to understand the doctrine of redemption. However, it is important to realize that our redemption can only be through the Son of God, because He was the only Perfect Sacrifice.

This narrative is about a rather ordinary couple who loved each other. Their love story is a mirror in which we can see the divine love of Christ for you and me.

Ruth 1:1-5

Now it came about in the days when the judges [a]governed, that there was a famine in the land. And a certain man of Bethlehem in Judah went to sojourn in the land of Moab [b]with his wife and his two sons. 2 The name of the man *was* Elimelech, and the name of his wife, Naomi; and the names of his two sons *were* Mahlon and Chilion, Ephrathites of Bethlehem in Judah. Now they entered the land of Moab and remained there. 3 Then Elimelech, Naomi's husband, died; and she was left with her two sons. 4 They took for themselves Moabite women *as* wives; the name of the one was Orpah and the name of the other Ruth. And they lived there about ten years. 5 Then [c]both Mahlon and Chilion also died, and the woman was bereft of her two children and her husband.

Elimelech and his family left their home in Bethlehem because of a famine. The fact that his hometown was Bethlehem is important since the story of Ruth ends there. The events in this narrative had to take place for Christ to be born in Bethlehem some 1,000 years later.

While in Moab, Elimelech died and Naomi was left a widow. Later both their sons, Mahlon and Chilion, died.

Ruth 1:8-10

And Naomi said to her two daughters- in-law, "Go, return each of you to her mother's house. May the Lord deal kindly with you as you have dealt with the dead and with me. 9 May the Lord grant that you may find rest, each in the house of her husband." Then she kissed them, and they lifted up their voices and wept. 10 And they said to her, "*No*, but we will surely return with you to your people."

---

a. Ruth 1:1 Or *judged*; b. Lit *he, and*
c. Ruth 1:5 Lit *both of them*

Naomi decided to return to Bethlehem, and advised her daughters-in-law to return to their mothers' homes. But Ruth insisted that she would not leave Naomi. Rather, she would go with Naomi to Bethlehem. She had made an important decision – one that would affect the whole world. Most importantly, Ruth's decision would affect the genealogy of Christ. It was a decision for God.

Ruth 1:22

> So Naomi returned, and with her Ruth the Moabitess, her daughter-in-law, who returned from the land of Moab. And they came to Bethlehem at the beginning of barley harvest.

Harvest was a good time to arrive in Bethlehem.

Ruth 2:1

> Now Naomi had [a]a kinsman of her husband, a [b]man of great wealth, of the family of Elimelech, whose name was Boaz.

Here we are introduced to Boaz, who might be considered the hero of this story. Scripture indicates that he was affluent, a mighty man – a warrior of high repute, and a member of the family of Elimelech.

Ruth 2:2

> And Ruth the Moabitess said to Naomi, "Please let me go to the field and glean among the ears of grain after one in whose sight I may find favor." And she said to her, "Go, my daughter."

In this verse we learn of a law which is somewhat strange to us – the law of gleaning. The ability to glean (harvest) grain or produce was God's way of taking care of the poor. It was a part of the Mosaic system.

---

a. Ruth 2:1 Or *an acquaintance*; b. Or *mighty, valiant man*

Leviticus 19:9-10

'Now when you reap the harvest of your land, you shall not reap to the very corners of your field, nor shall you gather the gleanings of your harvest. 10 Nor shall you glean your vineyard, nor shall you gather the fallen fruit of your vineyard; you shall leave them for the needy and for the stranger. I am the LORD your God.

The grain in the corners of the fields, and what was missed in the first harvest, was left for the poor and for strangers. This law also applied to the vineyards.

Ruth 2:3-7

So she departed and went and gleaned in the field after the reapers; and [a]she happened to come to the portion of the field belonging to Boaz, who was of the family of Elimelech. 4 Now behold, Boaz came from Bethlehem and said to the reapers, "May the LORD be with you." And they said to him, "May the LORD bless you." 5 Then Boaz said to his servant who was [b]in charge of the reapers, "Whose young woman is this?" 6 The servant [c]in charge of the reapers replied, "She is the young Moabite woman who returned with Naomi from the land of Moab. 7 And she said, 'Please let me glean and gather after the reapers among the sheaves.' Thus she came and has remained from the morning until now; she has been sitting in the house for a little while."

Ruth entered a field to glean. As Scripture points out, the field belonged to Boaz. When Boaz arrived, he saw Ruth and asked her identity of the servant in charge. The servant told him that she was Naomi's daughter-in-law, a Moabitess, who had asked permission to glean.

Boaz had more than a passing interest in Ruth.

---

a. Ruth 2:3 Lit *her chance chanced upon*
b. Ruth 2:5 Lit *appointed over*
c. Ruth 2:6 Lit *who was appointed over*

Ruth 2:8
> Then Boaz said to Ruth, "[a]Listen carefully, my daughter. Do not go to glean in another field; furthermore, do not go on from this one, but stay here with my maids.

Most owners did not want gleaners (the poor) in their fields and vineyards. Only because it was Mosaic Law was gleaning permitted. Boaz invited Ruth to glean in his field, further showing his interest in the young woman.

Ruth 2:10
> Then she fell on her face, bowing to the ground and said to him, "Why have I found favor in your sight that you should take notice of me, since I am a foreigner?"

Ruth was surprised to be treated so well by Boaz and his servants. The Moabite people were generally held in very low esteem. The Mosaic Law even shut Moabites out of the congregation of the Lord.

Ruth 2:11-12
> Boaz replied to her, "All that you have done for your mother-in-law after the death of your husband has been fully reported to me, and how you left your father and your mother and the land of your birth, and came to a people that you did not previously know. 12 May the LORD reward your work, and your wages be full from the LORD, the God of Israel, under whose wings you have come to seek refuge."

Boaz knew how Ruth had stood by Naomi, leaving her native land and moving to an unknown land. He realized the huge sacrifice she had made.

---

a. Ruth 2:8 Lit *Have you not heard*

Ruth had come to trust God, stating in Ruth 1:16, "Your people *shall be* my people, and your God, my God."

Ruth 2:14-16

At mealtime Boaz said to her, "[a]Come here, that you may eat of the bread and dip your piece of bread in the vinegar." So she sat beside the reapers; and he [b]served her roasted grain, and she ate and was satisfied and had some left. 15 When she rose to glean, Boaz commanded his servants, saying, "Let her glean even among the sheaves, and do not insult her. 16 Also you shall purposely pull out for her *some grain* from the bundles and leave *it* that she may glean, and do not rebuke her."

Boaz invited Ruth to dine with him. He also gave his reapers some very interesting instructions, which insured that her gleaning would be highly fruitful.

Ruth 2:20

Naomi said to her daughter-in-law, "May he be blessed of the LORD who has not withdrawn his kindness to the living and to the dead." Again Naomi said to her, "The man is [c]our relative, he is one of our [d]closest relatives."

We see the providence of God here, not only in Ruth's successful gleaning, but in the fact that of all the fields in the area, she gleaned in a field of Boaz – a close relative who could fulfill the role of kinsman-redeemer.

There were three basic applications in the Mosaic Law related to a kinsman-redeemer. The first application concerned the land. If a person sold their land, it would be returned to them in the year of Jubilee – the 50th year. But if a wealthy relative (kinsman)

---

a. Ruth 2:14 Lit *Draw near*; b. Lit *held out to*
c. Ruth 2:20 Lit *near to us*; d. Lit *redeemers*

could pay this debt off ahead of time – the land could be "redeemed" early and returned to the original owner. The second application concerned slavery. Extremely poor persons sometimes sold themselves into servitude (or slavery). As an indentured servant, they were required to work for a certain number of years to "buy back" their freedom. A kinsman-redeemer could pay this debt early to free their relative from slavery. The third and perhaps most interesting application of the kinsman-redeemer law related to widows. Under The Law, a widowed woman's deceased husband's closest male relative could marry her. The kinsman-redeemer could be a brother, uncle, cousin, or other close male relative. In this case, one other eligible kinsman declined the role, leaving Boaz next in line. The kinsman-redeemer concept is a perfect picture of Christ redeeming us at the Cross.

Ruth 3:1-2
Then Naomi her mother-in-law said to her, "My daughter, shall I not seek [a]security for you, that it may be well with you? 2 Now is not Boaz our [b]kinsman, with whose maids you were? Behold, he winnows barley at the threshing floor tonight.

Evidently Ruth was very modest, and made no claim on Boaz, even though he had shown a great deal of interest. Naomi, having observed Boaz's interest, advised Ruth of the way to claim Boaz as kinsman-redeemer.

---

a. Ruth 3:1 Lit *rest*
b. Ruth 3:2 Or *acquaintance*

Ruth 3:4-9

It shall be when he lies down, that you shall [a]notice the place where he lies, and you shall go and uncover his feet and lie down; then he will tell you what you shall do." 5 She said to her, "All that you say I will do." 6 So she went down to the threshing floor and did according to all that her mother-in-law had commanded her. 7 When Boaz had eaten and drunk and his heart was merry, he went to lie down at the end of the heap of grain; and she came secretly, and uncovered his feet and lay down. 8 It happened in the middle of the night that the man was startled and [b]bent forward; and behold, a woman was lying at his feet. 9 He said, "Who are you?" And she answered, "I am Ruth your maid. So spread your covering over your maid, for you are a [c]close relative."

Nothing was improper about what happened on the threshing floor. This was an accepted practice in claiming a kinsman-redeemer, and it took place in a public area.

Ruth 3:10

Then he said, "May you be blessed of the Lord, my daughter. You have shown your last kindness to be better than the first by not going after young men, whether poor or rich.

Obviously Boaz was overjoyed that Ruth had not been "husband hunting." Chiefly because of the wise advice of Naomi, Ruth had followed a non-obtrusive path to naming Boaz as her kinsman-redeemer – rather than publicly claiming him before the elders of the city (which was also acceptable according to Mosaic Law).

Ruth's approach was wise, in effect giving Boaz a choice of saying yes or no.

---

a. Ruth 3:4 Lit *know*
b. Ruth 3:8 Lit *twisted himself*
c. Ruth 3:9 Or *redeemer*

Ruth 4:13-14

So Boaz took Ruth, and she became his wife, and he went in to her. And the LORD [a]enabled her to conceive, and she gave birth to a son. 14 Then the women said to Naomi, "Blessed is the Lord who has not left you without a [b]redeemer today, and may his name [c]become famous in Israel.

The women rejoiced with Naomi, praising the LORD for this kinsman. Naomi needed a kinsman to carry on the line of Elimelech, and now this had been accomplished. Little did any of these people realize how important this link was in the line of Judah, and in the eventual birth of Christ.

Ruth 4:17

The neighbor women gave him a name, saying, "A son has been born to Naomi!" So they named him Obed. He is the father of Jesse, the father of David.

Naomi's neighbors noticed her great love for this child, whose name was Obed (which meant servant or worshiper). Obed was of no blood kin to Naomi, but he was legally her grandson since Ruth was her daughter-in-law. Most likely Obed took care of Naomi in her old age, since he was her legal heir, assuming the role left vacant by the death of her husband and two sons.

Obed was a worshiper of God; the true and living God. He was in the line of Judah, and was the grandfather of King David.

---

a. Ruth 4:13 Lit *gave her conception*
b. Ruth 4:14 Or *closest relative*; c. Lit *be called in*

CHAPTER 14: DAVID ANOINTED

Here we will become familiar with David, the second king of Israel. In the previous chapter of 1 Samuel (Chapter 15), God had taken the kingdom from David's father-in-law, Saul, because of his disobedience. Saul and David were very different. David was God's man. Saul was Satan's man. To bear this out, notice in 1 Samuel 15:25, when Saul asked Samuel to intervene with God for him. In at least two instances Saul said, "the LORD *your* God." He did not say, "the LORD *my* God" or "the LORD *our* God."

1 Samuel 15:21-26

But the people took *some* of the spoil, sheep and oxen, the choicest of the things devoted to destruction, to sacrifice to the LORD your God at Gilgal." 22 Samuel said,

"Has the LORD as much delight in
burnt offerings and sacrifices
As in obeying the voice of the LORD?
Behold, to obey is better than sacrifice,
And to heed than the fat of rams.
23 "For rebellion is as the sin of divination,
And insubordination is as iniquity and idolatry.
Because you have rejected the word of the LORD, He
has also rejected you from *being* king."

24 Then Saul said to Samuel, "I have sinned; I have indeed transgressed the [a]command of the LORD and your words, because I feared the people and listened to their voice. 25 Now therefore, please pardon my sin and return with me, that I may worship the LORD." 26 But Samuel said to Saul, "I will not return with you; for you have rejected the word of the LORD, and the LORD has rejected you from being king over Israel."

---

a. 1 Samuel 15:24 Lit *mouth*

1 Samuel 15:27-30

As Samuel turned to go, *Saul* seized the edge of his robe, and it tore. 28 So Samuel said to him, "The LORD has torn the kingdom of Israel from you today and has given it to your neighbor, who is better than you. 29 Also the [a]Glory of Israel will not lie or change His mind; for He is not a man that He should change His mind." 30 Then he said, "I have sinned; *but* please honor me now before the elders of my people and before Israel, and go back with me, that I may worship the LORD your God."

God had ordered extreme surgery in the slaying of the Amalekites and King Agag. Saul deliberately disobeyed God's instructions to completely destroy the Amalekites (King Agag, the men, women, children and animals). Instead, he did not kill Agag, and he kept the choicest animals.

Amalek was the son of Esau. The Amalekites fought the children of Israel to prevent them from entering the promised land. God said He would make war with Amalek from generation to generation, and would finally judge the Amalekites. They had been given about 500 years to change their ways, but because they had definitely turned their backs on God, He did judge and destroy them.

God had chosen David to succeed Saul, and sent Samuel to Bethlehem to anoint David as king.

1 Samuel 16:1

Now the Lord said to Samuel, "How long will you grieve over Saul, since I have rejected him from being king over Israel? Fill your horn with oil and go; I will send you to Jesse the Bethlehemite, for I have selected a king for Myself among his sons."

---

a. 1 Samuel 15:29 Or *Eminence*

Saul had Samuel, who seemed to like him a great deal more than he liked David, on his side. Samuel was grieved to have to bring Saul the bad news that the kingdom was to be taken from him. Samuel's sorrow makes Saul's rejection by God much more poignant.

1 Samuel 16:2-3

But Samuel said, "How can I go? When Saul hears of *it*, he will kill me." And the LORD said, "Take a heifer with you and say, 'I have come to sacrifice to the LORD.' 3 You shall invite Jesse to the sacrifice, and I will show you what you shall do; and you shall anoint for Me the one whom I [a]designate to you."

Samuel was desperately afraid to go to Jesse. He knew Saul's nature, and he also knew Saul was in no mood for opposition. God had chosen the next king, and gave Samuel specific instructions. But He did not reveal to Samuel any other advance information about His choice. (Perhaps the old saying, "What you don't know won't hurt you," applies here.) As instructed, Samuel went to Bethlehem and requested that Jesse and his sons come for a sacrifice.

1 Samuel 16:6-7

When they entered, he looked at Eliab and thought, "Surely the LORD's anointed is before Him." 7 But the LORD said to Samuel, "Do not look at his appearance or at the height of his stature, because I have rejected him; for [b]God *sees* not as man sees, for man looks at the outward appearance, but the LORD looks at the heart."

When Samuel looked at Eliab, he saw a handsome, strong young man, and was sure this was God's choice for the next king of Israel. However, God cautioned

---

a. 1 Samuel 16:3 Lit *say to you*
b. 1 Samuel 16:7 So with Gr; Heb He does *not see what man sees*

Samuel not to look at the outward appearance – not to judge Eliab by his looks. God told Samuel that He would select the king this time. Certainly God could make a better judgment than Samuel.

We all have a tendency to judge people – even in our Christian circles – by appearance, financial status, education, clothes, fancy cars, large homes, careers, and social position. God never judges people on these characteristics, but rather examines the heart.

1 Samuel 16:10-11

Thus Jesse made seven of his sons pass before Samuel. But Samuel said to Jesse, "The LORD has not chosen these." 11 And Samuel said to Jesse, "Are these all the children?" And he said, "There remains yet the youngest, and behold, he is tending the sheep." Then Samuel said to Jesse, "Send and [a]bring him; for we will not sit down until he comes here."

As the seven eldest sons passed before Samuel, he told Jesse that the LORD had not chosen any of them. Apparently Jesse never thought his youngest son, David, would be considered – he was just a boy, only about 16 years old. He was a herder of sheep, out tending the flock during this selection process. But Samuel insisted on seeing David, and would not rest until he had accomplished his mission.

1 Samuel 16:12

So he sent and brought him in. Now he was ruddy, with beautiful eyes and a handsome appearance. And the LORD said, "Arise, anoint him; for this is he."

This Scripture describes David as being ruddy (red-headed), with a nice countenance. As we read more

---

a. 1 Samuel 16:11 Lit *take*

about David we find that at times he did display a hot temper – a characteristic often attributed to redheads. David was a very handsome young man, but God did not choose him for that reason. God looked upon David's heart and made His choice. God knew everything there was to know about David; He sees what we cannot see. As we study further, we learn that David failed at times. Yet with all his physical failures, his faith never failed. David loved and trusted God, despite being punished by God for his wrongdoings. He remained the apple of God's eye, and God loved him dearly.

1 Samuel 16:13
Then Samuel took the horn of oil and anointed him in the midst of his brothers; and the Spirit of the LORD came mightily upon David from that day forward. And Samuel arose and went to Ramah.

The LORD'S Spirit came upon David when Samuel anointed him king of Israel. As this occurred, the Spirit of the LORD departed from Saul.

1 Samuel 16:14-16
Now the Spirit of the LORD departed from Saul, and an evil spirit from the LORD terrorized him. 15 Saul's servants then said to him, "Behold now, an evil spirit from God is terrorizing you. 16 Let our lord now command your servants who are before you. Let them seek a man who is a skillful player on the harp; and it shall come about when the evil spirit from God is on you, that he shall play *the harp* with his hand, and you will be well."

When the LORD'S Spirit departed from Saul, it is very possible that he was completely taken over by Satan. His servants noted that Saul had a mental problem, a malady believed to be nothing more than a spiritual sickness. It has been said that music has the power to tame the savage beast. Saul's servants suggested a search for a good musician.

1 Samuel 16:17-23

So Saul said to his servants, "Provide for me now a man who can play well and bring *him* to me." 18 Then one of the young men said, "Behold, I have seen a son of Jesse the Bethlehemite who is a skillful musician, a mighty man of valor, a warrior, one prudent in speech, and a handsome man; and the LORD is with him." 19 So Saul sent messengers to Jesse and said, "Send me your son David who is with the flock." 20 Jesse took a donkey *loaded with* bread and a jug of wine and a young goat, and sent *them* to Saul by David his son. 21 Then David came to Saul and [a]attended him; and [b]Saul loved him greatly, and he became his armor bearer. 22 Saul sent to Jesse, saying, "Let David now stand before me, for he has found favor in my sight." 23 So it came about whenever the *evil* spirit from God came to Saul, David would take the harp and play *it* with his hand; and Saul would be refreshed and be well, and the evil spirit would depart from him.

David, who was a very talented musician, was recommended and brought into the palace. Saul was forsaken of God, and David was brought to court to soothe Saul by playing the harp.

Throughout 1 Samuel we discover excellent spiritual principles. For instance, in 1 Samuel 15:22, Samuel said to Saul, "to obey is better than sacrifice, *And* to heed than the fat of rams." We demonstrate whether or not we are children of the Lord Jesus Christ by our love for Him. This is not by what we say in a testimony, but whether or not we are obeying Him. To be a Christian is

---

a. 1 Samuel 16:21 Lit *stood before him*; b. Lit *he*

to live a life of trust and obedience. It is not something to do in ritual and pretense. When God looks at us, He sees our heart. He looks at the inner person when He selects someone for a particular task. We cannot hide anything from Him – He always checks the interior.

CHAPTER 15: DAVID IS PROMISED AN ETERNAL THRONE

David's wish had been to build God a temple. At first Nathan, a prophet of God, told David to proceed; however, in a dream that same night, God instructed Nathan differently. David had killed many men during battles, and had caused the death of Uriah. God did not want David to build the temple because his hands were stained with too much blood. Instead, God promised that He would build David a house. As we study further, we will see that this House was to be God's eternal Kingdom, governed in the end times by none other than our Lord and Savior, Jesus Christ.

2 Samuel 7:12
When your days are complete and you lie down with your fathers, I will raise up your [a]descendant after you, who will come forth from [b]you, and I will establish his kingdom.

What wonderful news! Again, the promise was repeated. We read in the New Testament that the Lord Jesus Christ was born a descendant of David.

Romans 1:3
concerning His Son, who was born of a [c]descendant of David according to the flesh,

God was referring not to Solomon here, but rather to the Lord Jesus Christ.

2 Samuel 7:13
He shall build a house for My name, and I will establish the throne of his kingdom forever.

---

a. 2 Samuel 7:12 Lit *seed*; b. Lit *your bowels*
c. Romans 1:3 Lit *seed*

Solomon was next in line for the throne, but the Kingdom referred to here goes far beyond Solomon, to the future. The angel Gabriel's message to Mary confirms that the Lord Jesus Christ will one day be seated on the throne of David.

Luke 1:32
> He will be great and will be called the Son of the Most High; and the Lord God will give Him the throne of His father David;

2 Samuel 7:14
> I will be a father to him and he will be a son to Me; when he commits iniquity, I will correct him with the rod of men and the strokes of the sons of men,

This passage describes the unique relationship between God and the Lord Jesus Christ, which is not the same as human father-son relationships. The last part of this verse seems very strange. A better translation, from Bishop Samuel Horsley, an 18th century Anglican, is "When guilt is laid upon him, I will chasten him with the rod of men."

In other words, God said that when our guilt is laid on Jesus, 'I'm going to be his Father and He will be my Son.' God would punish Jesus instead of punishing us. That is the unique relationship between God the Father and God the Son. He has borne your sins and my sins, and paid with His life when He died on the Cross for you and me.

Isaiah 53:5
> But He was [a]pierced through for our transgressions. He was crushed for our iniquities; The chastening for our [b]well-being *fell* upon Him, And by His scourging we are healed.

---

a. Isaiah 53:5 Or *wounded*; b. Or *peace*

John 20:17
> Jesus *said to her, "Stop clinging to Me, for I have not yet ascended to the Father; but go to My brethren and say to them, 'I ascend to My Father and your Father, and My God and your God.'"

At His resurrection, the Lord Jesus Christ spoke to Mary Magdalene about His ascension, again confirming that He is the Son of God.

John 1:12
> But as many as received Him, to them He gave the right to become children of God, *even* to those who believe in His name,

Upon receiving Christ as your personal Savior, because of God's position in the Trinity, you become a child of God.

2 Samuel 7:15
> but My lovingkindness shall not depart from him, as I took *it* away from Saul, whom I removed from before you.

In spite of the line of David sinning grievously, God carried out His promise and purpose with David and his line. He brought the Lord Jesus Christ into the world.

2 Samuel 7:16
> Your house and your kingdom shall endure before [a]Me forever; your throne shall be established forever.'"'"

This promise was so important that God repeated it several times throughout Scripture.

---

a. 2 Samuel 7:16 So with Gr and some ancient mss; M.T. *you*

Psalm 89:34-37

"My covenant I will not [a]violate, Nor will I alter [b]the utterance of My lips. 35 "[c]Once I have sworn by My holiness; I will not lie to David.
36 "His [d]descendants shall endure forever
And his throne as the sun before Me.
37 "It shall be established forever like the moon,
And the witness in the sky is faithful." [e]*Selah*.

God made a covenant with David, and God's covenant is assured. He will not break it.

---

a. Psalm 89:34 Lit *profane*; b. Lit *that which goes forth*
c. Psalm 89:35 Or *One thing*
d. Psalm 89:36 Lit *seed*
e. Psalm 89:37 *Selah* may mean: *Pause, Crescendo* or *Musical interlude*

CHAPTER 16: THE PROMISE IS REPEATED TO SOLOMON

1 Kings 9:5

> then I will establish the throne of your kingdom over Israel forever, just as I [a]promised to your father David, saying, '[b]You shall not lack a man on the throne of Israel.'

God charged Solomon in the verse before this, encouraging him to walk in the way that David his father had walked. We know that David had his problems; he was not perfect, yet he was loved greatly by God. He failed, fumbled and faltered throughout his life. But he always came back to God. He confessed his sins and asked for forgiveness – and God forgave him.

As long as Israel had a king, God kept one of the line of David on that throne. Now, today, there is One in David's line who sits at the right hand of God – whose nail-pierced hands hold the scepter of this universe.

---

a. 1 Kings 9:5 Lit *spoke*; b. Lit *There shall not be cut off to you a man*

CHAPTER 17: MY REDEEMER LIVES

Satan (through Job's friends) had brought Job to the place where he was not yet humbled, but still trying to vindicate himself before God. Job had suffered both mental and physical anguish. He had lost everything, including all of his family – with the exception of his loving wife who advised him to "curse God and die."

Despite his desperation, Job uttered one of the greatest affirmations of love in the Bible. He was ready to die under the discipline of Almighty God. Feeling the pain of the lash on his back, still he yearned for God.

Job 19:25-27

"As for me, I know that my [a]Redeemer lives, And [b]at the last He will take His stand on the [c]earth. 26 "Even after my skin [d]is destroyed, Yet from my flesh I shall see God; 27 Whom I [e]myself shall behold, And whom my eyes will see and not another. My [f]heart faints [g]within me!

Job had been extremely ill, and was in a state of shock from all of his troubles. All he wanted to do was die – not the eternal death, but rather the physical death which would provide relief from his turbulence and sorrow. Job knew he would be raised again, and that in his restored body he would see his Redeemer.

Job very correctly believed in the resurrection of the dead. The bodies of the dead in Christ – believers who die before the return of Christ – will be returned to dust, but their souls will go to be with Christ immediately. When Christ returns, our bodies will be resurrected. This is a very wonderful promise to a Christian.

---

a. Job 19:25 Or *Vindicator, defender;* lit *kinsman;* b. Or *as the Last;* c. Lit *dust*
d. Job 19:26 Lit *which they have cut off*
e. Job 19:27 Or *on my side;* f. Lit *kidneys;* g. Lit *in my loins*

CHAPTER 18: THE LORD'S ANOINTED

What is a Psalm? In Hebrew, Psalms means *Praises* or *Book of Praises*. The Greek word *Psalmos* suggests something musical – an instrumental accompaniment. It is the Jewish Book of Worship – the hymn book of the temple. It is the "Him-Book" – all about HIM, yet most of Psalms was written about 1000 BC.

The Book of Psalms contains much more about Christ than we will cover, but let's begin with Psalm 2.

Psalm 2:1
Why are the [a]nations in an uproar
And the peoples devising a vain thing?

The Gentile (heathen) nations rage, and the Jewish people plot a vain, empty thing. That which has made the Gentiles so mad – and has brought together mankind in a great protest movement – is a mass turning away from God and His Anointed.

We see this happening today with the removal of anything pertaining to God, the Bible, and prayer from our public schools, institutions of higher learning, businesses, and government buildings. The public sector and many businesses now forbid the mere mention of God in the workplace. The Ten Commandments have been removed from display in public places. The list goes on and on.

All of these changes reflect the vain, futile attempts of man to deny the existence of God and His Son. Yet God does exist, now and forever. Man's denial of Him certainly does not change the fact of His existence.

---

a. Psalm 2:1 Or *Gentiles*

Psalm 2:2
> The kings of the earth take their stand
> And the rulers take counsel together
> Against the LORD and against His [a]Anointed, *saying*,

The kings of the earth, the political and religious rulers, guide and advise each other. The establishment (government) joined forces with the general population in this protest movement to create a very unusual situation. Consider that Herod, Pilate, the high priest Caiaphas, the scribes, the Pharisees, the people of Israel, and the Gentiles were all gathered together for the sole purpose of putting Christ to death. These factions were opposed to each other under ordinary situations.

What are they protesting? And who are they against? They are against God and His Anointed. The word "Anointed" is translated *Messiah* from the Hebrew. The Greek New Testament translation is *Christos*, and in English, *Christ*.

The first persecution of the Church was recorded in the Chapter 4 of Acts. After being threatened, the apostles Peter and John returned to the church at Jerusalem and delivered their report.

Acts 4:24
> And when they heard *this*, they lifted their voices to God with one accord and said, "O [b]Lord, it is YOU WHO MADE THE HEAVEN AND THE EARTH AND THE SEA, AND ALL THAT IS IN THEM,

The early Church had no questions or misgivings about their beliefs. Today there are a growing number of churches who do not claim that the LORD is God. They are not even sure God is God. There is a great deal

---

a. Psalm 2:2 Or *Messiah*
b. Acts 4:24 Or *Master*

of uncertainty and confusion among church members. This movement against God has been snowballing down through the centuries, and in the end times will result in a worldwide revolt against God and Christ.

Revelation 19:19
And I saw the beast and the kings of the earth and their armies assembled to make war against Him who sat on the horse and against His army.

Psalm 2:3
"Let us tear their fetters apart
And cast away their cords from us!"

We should not wonder what fetters means. Just review the Ten Commandments to see some of them. From the beginning, starting with Adam and Eve, God has placed limitations on the human family.

Genesis 2:24
For this reason a man shall leave his father and his mother, and be joined to his wife; and they shall become one flesh.

He made marriage (one of the cords) for the welfare of all people, whether or not Christian. God gave marriage to mankind, as a covenant between man and woman. Now mankind wants to grossly distort the definition of marriage, or even abolish it. God established the covenant of marriage, and He intended for it to be obeyed.

God has provided us with His policies and procedures in the form of the Holy Bible. All through the Bible He has explained *in detail* how we are to conduct ourselves in relation to Him and to each other. Today many say that we don't need the Ten Commandments – they are not applicable to modern day society. God authored them – they are the standards for life. He created them to protect mankind. All of our laws in the civilized world are based on these Ten Commandments. They serve as a guide for behavior – rules to live by – so people will not be completely lawless.

When we compare how we live to the Ten Commandments, we all fall short of God's standards. In both our political and business arenas, many of those who should be setting the example participate in all kinds of corruption, confusion, compromise, indifference, and bending of the rules to fit their circumstances.

In our social sphere, we find a very disturbing, burgeoning mindset. It is called "not accepting your responsibility." When laws are broken, or behavior is otherwise unacceptable, excuses are made to transfer the blame to medical, psychological, or childhood malady. Shifting blame to someone or something else has become an epidemic.

Psalm 2:4
> He who [a]sits in the heavens laughs,
> The Lord scoffs at them.

This behavior is not funny to God. He laughs at man's vain, futile aspirations. It will be settled in the end.

Psalm 2:5
> Then He will speak to them in His anger
> And terrify them in His fury, saying,

The Lord's judgment will be visited on the earth. It is not possible to successfully oppose God, or to deter Him from His plans.

---

a. Psalm 2:4 Or *is enthroned*

Psalm 2:6

"But as for Me, I have [a]installed My King
Upon Zion, My holy mountain."

God is undaunted, unhesitating, and uncompromising – always moving towards the establishment of Christ's throne. To us it seems that a great deal of time has elapsed since Christ ascended, but it is written in God's Word that a thousand years is as a day to Him. (2 Peter 3:8; Psalm 90:4) From that standpoint, it has only been two days.

Psalm 2:7

"I will surely tell of the [b]decree of the Lord:
He said to Me, 'You are My Son,
Today I have begotten You.

This reference is not speaking of the birth of the Lord Jesus Christ. He was never begotten in the sense of having a beginning. This is in reference to His resurrection. Christ was begotten (taken) out of Joseph of Arimathea's tomb. Jesus is the eternal Son of God, and God is the eternal Father. You cannot have an eternal Father without having an eternal Son. They are Father and Son throughout eternity. A good reference to prove this is found in Proverbs.

Proverbs 8:22

"The LORD possessed me at the beginning of His way,
Before His works [c]of old.

Psalm 2:8

'Ask of Me, and I will surely give the [d]nations as
Your inheritance, And the *very* ends of the earth as
Your possession.

---

a. Psalm 2:6 Or *consecrated*
b. Psalm 2:7 Or *decree: The LORD said to Me*
c. Proverbs 8:22 Lit *from then*
d. Psalm 2:8 Or *Gentiles*

Jesus holds the scepter of the universe in His nail-scarred hands. This verse is often used in missionary conferences; however, it does not have anything to do with missions, as the next verse explains.

Psalm 2:9
'You shall [a]break them with a [b]rod of iron,
You shall shatter them like [c]earthenware.'"

This passage does not reference Christ's First Coming, but speaks of His Second Coming – when He returns to the earth as Judge. He has not asked anyone to apologize for Him, and we should not apologize. Christ said that He intends to come and quell the rebellion with a rod of iron. This is very different than when He came to earth some 2,000 years ago, the man of Galilee, the carpenter of Nazareth, the gentle Jesus.

Can you imagine what would happen if Jesus were to say to the head of North Korea, "I'm Jesus, I'm here to take over?" Do you think they would say, "We've been waiting for you?"

Or what if He went to Rome, to the Vatican, and said to the Pope, "I'm here to take over." Do you think He would be received as Savior of the world and as King of the universe – the Almighty King? The reaction would more likely be, "Now look, you've come a little too soon. We're having trouble with some of our priests, but we're trying to work that out so we don't need you."

When Jesus comes to earth this second time He will be the Absolute Monarch. It will be a one-person rule, the Perfect Dictatorship.

---

a. Psalm 2:9 Another reading is *rule*; b. Or *scepter* or *staff*; c. Lit *potter's ware*

CHAPTER 19: HIS RESURRECTION

Psalm 16:8-10

> I have set the LORD continually before me; Because He is at my right hand, I will not be shaken. 9 Therefore my heart is glad and my glory rejoices; My flesh also will dwell securely. 10 For You will not abandon my soul to [a]Sheol; Nor will You [b]allow Your [c]Holy One to [d]undergo decay.

This prophecy of David was quoted by Peter in his sermon on the Day of Pentecost.

Acts 2:25-30

> For David says of Him,
>
> > 'I SAW THE LORD ALWAYS IN MY PRESENCE;
> > FOR HE IS AT MY RIGHT HAND, SO THAT I WILL NOT BE SHAKEN. 26 'THEREFORE MY HEART WAS GLAD AND MY TONGUE EXULTED; MOREOVER MY FLESH ALSO WILL LIVE IN HOPE; 27 BECAUSE YOU WILL NOT ABANDON MY SOUL TO HADES, NOR [e]ALLOW YOUR [f]HOLY ONE TO [g]UNDERGO DECAY. 28 'YOU HAVE MADE KNOWN TO ME THE WAYS OF LIFE; YOU WILL MAKE ME FULL OF GLADNESS WITH YOUR PRESENCE.'
>
> 29 "[h]Brethren, I may confidently say to you regarding the patriarch David that he both died and was buried, and his tomb is [i]with us to this day. 30 And so, because he was a prophet and knew that GOD HAD SWORN TO HIM WITH AN OATH TO SEAT *one* [j]OF HIS DESCENDANTS ON HIS THRONE,

---

a. Psalm 16:10 I.e. the nether world; b. Lit *give*; c. Or *godly one*;
d. Or *see corruption* or *the pit*
e. Acts 2:27 Lit *give*; f. Or *devout* or *pious*; g. Lit *see corruption*
h. Acts 2:29 Lit *Men brothers*; i. Lit *among*
j. Acts 2:30 Lit *of the fruit of his loins*

Acts 2:31-33

he looked ahead and spoke of the resurrection of [a]the Christ, that HE WAS NEITHER ABANDONED TO HADES, NOR DID His flesh [b]SUFFER DECAY. 32 This Jesus God raised up again, to which we are all witnesses. 33 Therefore having been exalted [c]to the right hand of God, and having received from the Father the promise of the Holy Spirit, He has poured forth this which you both see and hear.

Peter gives us a full explanation of these verses from Psalm 16. Many people think that this passage is about David. Note the statement, "Because He is at my right hand," (Psalm 16:8). David was highly esteemed, but he doesn't sit at the right hand of God. Further, notice, "Nor will You allow Your Holy One to undergo decay." (Psalm 16:10) David did not consider himself a Holy One. This was all about the resurrection of Jesus Christ.

---

a. Acts 2:31 I.e. the Messiah; b. Lit *see corruption*
c. Acts 2:33 Or *by*

CHAPTER 20: THE SHEPHERD'S PSALMS

The next three Psalms covered in this study are referred to as the Shepherd's Psalms. Throughout the Bible, God's people are called sheep. The distinctive characteristic of sheep is that they must be cared for – fed, watered, protected. Left on their own sheep will not survive, just as we will not survive in the long-term without the Shepherd described in these wonderful Shepherd's Psalms.

Psalm 22: He is the Good Shepherd who died for His sheep.

John 10:11
"I am the good shepherd; the good shepherd lays down His life for the sheep.

Jesus provided the ultimate sacrifice – the only sacrifice acceptable to God – so we may have eternal life.

Psalm 23: He is the Great Shepherd.

He is living, and has fulfilled this Perfect Sacrifice. He is leading us beside the still waters. He goes with us through the valley of the shadow of death, providing us with a feeling of safety, because we have placed our confidence in Him. We have an assurance that we will dwell in the house of the Lord forever.

Psalm 24: He is our sovereign King.

He will come back as Judge and sovereign King. His Kingdom will be forever and ever – a Kingdom of righteousness.

John 10:14-15

I am the good shepherd, and I know My own and My own know Me, 15 even as the Father knows Me and I know the Father; and I lay down My life for the sheep.

Revelation 7:17

for the Lamb in the center of the throne will be their shepherd, and will guide them to springs of the [a]water of life; and God will wipe every tear from their eyes.

---

a. Revelation 7:17 Lit *waters*

CHAPTER 21: CRUCIFIXION OF CHRIST

Bear in mind as we study Psalm 22 that this was written by David around 1000 BC – 1,000 years *before* Christ came to the earth. Perhaps we should call this the "Psalm of the Cross" because it describes very clearly and concisely the Crucifixion of Christ, more so than any other portion of the Word of God. It corresponds to the 22nd chapter of Genesis and the 53rd chapter of Isaiah. Psalm 22 provides an x-ray view which penetrates into Christ's thoughts – His innermost thoughts. In this Psalm we see the anguish of His passion. His soul is laid bare.

In the gospels (Matthew, Mark, Luke, John), the historical fact of Jesus' death is recorded along with some events surrounding His Crucifixion, but only in Psalm 22 are His thoughts revealed. Here we find an extraordinarily vivid "mind's eye" view of Jesus as He was hanging there – what went on in His heart and soul as He was suspended between heaven and earth on the Cross. He became a ladder let down from heaven to this earth so that men might have a way to reach God.

Psalm 22:1
A Cry of Anguish and a Song of Praise.
For the choir director; upon [a]Aijeleth Hashshahar.
A Psalm of David.

> My God, my God, why have You forsaken me?
> [b]Far from my deliverance are the words of my [c]groaning.

There has been an attempt to downplay the reality – the bitter truth – that Christ was forsaken of God. Some scholars take the position that Jesus was not forsaken,

---

a. Psalm 22:1 Lit *the hind of the morning*; b. Or Why are You so *far from helping me*, and from *the words of my groaning?* c. Lit *roaring*

attempting to translate His words in another way; however, translations of the Hebrew, Aramaic, and Greek languages all make it very clear that He *was* forsaken of God.

Hebrews 2:9
> But we do see Him who was made [a]for a little while lower than the angels, *namely*, Jesus, because of the suffering of death crowned with glory and honor, so that by the grace of God He might taste death for everyone.

Yes! He was made a man. And why? Jesus left His throne in Heaven's glory and became a man – to reveal God to mankind – but most of all to redeem mankind. He can save no one by His life or His teaching. It was His sacrifice – the Perfect Sacrifice – that could deliver mankind from sin. But as Christ called out to God, He was abandoned by God, and there was no place to turn. The human aspect had deserted Him, and the Divine (as we will see in the next Scripture) had abandoned Him. He was forsaken.

Psalm 22:3
> Yet You are holy, O You who [b]are enthroned upon the praises of Israel.

Why was He forsaken of God? Because on the Cross, in those last three hours, in the impenetrable darkness, He became sin for us. He was forsaken for what is only a brief moment to God. The paradox is at that very moment God was in Christ, reconciling the world unto Himself.

---

a. Hebrews 2:9 Or *a little lower*
b. Psalm 22:3 Or *inhabit the praises*

John 16:32

Behold, an hour is coming, and has *already* come, for you to be scattered, each to his own *home*, and to leave Me alone; and *yet* I am not alone, because the Father is with Me.

The Father was with Christ all through this ordeal. He was with Him when He was being scourged. He was with Him when He was nailed to the Cross. In those last three hours He became the sole offering for sin.

Isaiah 53:10

But the LORD was pleased To crush Him, [a]putting *Him* to grief; If [b]He would render Himself *as* a guilt offering, He will see *His* [c]offspring, He will prolong *His* days, And the [d]good pleasure of the LORD will prosper in His hand.

This further explains what Christ endured for us.

Isaiah 53:7

He was oppressed and He was afflicted, Yet He did not open His mouth; Like a lamb that is led to slaughter, And like a sheep that is silent before its shearers, So He did not open His mouth.

At His trial, He was silent.

Matthew 27:12-14

And while He was being accused by the chief priests and elders, He did not answer. 13 Then Pilate *said to Him, "Do You not hear how many things they testify against You?" 14 And He did not answer him with regard to even a *single* [e]charge, so the governor was quite amazed.

---

a. Isaiah 53:10 Lit *He made Him sick*; b. Lit *His soul*; c. Lit *seed*; d. Or *will of* e. Matthew 27:14 Lit *word*

When they scourged Him, He said nothing. When they nailed Him to the Cross, He did not whimper. But when God forsook Him, He roared like a lion – a roar of pain. His roaring was like a plaintive shriek; a wail of unutterable woe. The sins of the world were pressed down upon Him.

Psalm 22:6
But I am a worm and not a man,
A reproach of men and despised by the people.

What does it mean when He says He is a worm? He has roared like a lion, and now says, "I am a worm." The worm referred to here is a Crocus worm, which was used by the Hebrews in dyeing the curtains of the Tabernacle a rich, scarlet red.

Isaiah 53:3
He was despised and forsaken of men,
A man of [a]sorrows and acquainted with [b]grief;
And like one from whom men hide their face
He was despised, and we did not esteem Him.

When He said, "I am a worm," He meant more than that. His Spirit had reached the lowest level – the very lowest place.

Isaiah 1:18
"Come now, and let us reason together,"
Says the LORD, "Though your sins are as scarlet,
They will be as white as snow; Though they are red
like crimson, They will be like wool.

Only His blood can rub out that deep, dark spot in our lives. The blood of Jesus Christ, God's Son, cleanses us from all sin – but we must accept His sacrifice to receive this cleansing of sin.

---

a. Isaiah 53:3 Or *pains*; b. Or *sickness*

Psalm 22:7-8

All who see me [a]sneer at me; They [b]separate with the lip, they wag the head, *saying*,
8 "[c]Commit *yourself* to the LORD; let Him deliver him; Let Him rescue him, because He delights in him."

As we look at this victim on the Cross, we see His suffering magnified by that brutal mob – the hardened spectators gazing up at Him. In this Scripture we can look through the eyes of Christ and see what He saw.

Throughout history, some criminals have been so hated that they were taken from jail and lynched by angry mobs. After the hangings, the throngs would disperse – immediately cooled off and perhaps feeling shame.

Perhaps the lowest point in all of history was when this mob, as the Lord Jesus Christ was dying, watched Him suffer on the Cross. The terrible venom and vileness of the human heart was poured out like an open sewer, as the crowd watched and ridiculed Him in His death. Even a snake, after it bites and pours out its poison, slithers away in the grass. But not this crowd.

As Jesus looked out over the spectators, He saw not only the eyes of hate and antagonism, but He also saw some eyes of love. He saw His mother with John.

John 19:25

Therefore the soldiers did these things. But standing by the cross of Jesus were His mother, and His mother's sister, Mary the *wife* of Clopas, and Mary Magdalene.

---

a. Psalm 22:7 Or *mock me*; b. I.e. make mouths at me
c. Psalm 22:8 Lit *Roll*; another reading is *He committed* himself

Psalm 22:9-10

Yet You are He who brought me forth from the womb; You made me trust *when* upon my mother's breasts. 10 Upon You I was cast from [a]birth; You have been my God from my mother's womb.

John 19:26

When Jesus then saw His mother, and the disciple whom He loved standing nearby, He *said to His mother, "Woman, behold, your son!"

The first miracle Jesus performed was at a wedding in Cana, which is in Galilee. His mother asked Him to perform a miracle; something to show He was the Messiah. She wanted Him to reveal Himself.

John 2:4

And Jesus *said to her, "Woman, [b]what does that have to do with us? My hour has not yet come."

His answer to her indicated that the time was not appropriate for His true identity to be revealed. But as He hung on the Cross, He accomplished the most important work in the history of the world.

Psalm 22:12

Many bulls have surrounded me; Strong *bulls* of Bashan have encircled me.

This description of the very soldiers that crucified Christ – "bulls of Bashan" – brings to mind the idea of being devoured by wild animals, for that is what His tormenters had become.

---

a. Psalm 22:10 Lit *a womb*
b. John 2:4 Lit *what to Me and to you* (a Hebrew idiom)

Psalm 22:13
> They open wide their mouth at me,
> As a ravening and a roaring lion.

The Roman Empire, whose symbol was roaring lions, crucified Christ. Notice His condition in the next verse.

Psalm 22:14
> I am poured out like water, And all my bones are out of joint; My heart is like wax; It is melted within [a]me.

This happens to be a very accurate description of crucifixion. It is important to note that crucifixion was *totally unknown* when this Psalm was written. The Roman Empire, which instituted crucifixion, was not even in existence at this time. Yet here is a picture of a man dying by crucifixion.

"I am poured out like water," indicates excessive perspiration. "All my bones are out of joint," describes one of the more horrible aspects of crucifixion. As blood was lost, strength and muscle tone left, causing bones to slip out of joint – all part of the torture. It was a terrible, unimaginable suffering.

Indeed strange is the statement, "my heart is like wax." Christ died of a broken heart. Doctors have said that a ruptured heart would have produced what John meticulously recorded.

John 19:34
> But one of the soldiers pierced His side with a spear, and immediately blood and water came out.

---

a. Psalm 22:14 Lit *my inward parts*

Psalm 22:15
> My strength is dried up like a potsherd, And my tongue cleaves to my jaws; And You lay me [a]in the dust of death.

Hanging there, ready to expire, with excessive perspiration, He was very thirsty. Those beneath the Cross heard Him say, "I thirst."

Psalm 22:16
> For dogs have surrounded me; [b]A band of evildoers has encompassed me; [c]They pierced my hands and my feet.

The Roman soldiers, commonly referred to as dogs (a derogatory term for Gentiles) surrounded Him. All the sin and wickedness of mankind was upon Him, as His hands and feet were pierced. Again, described in detail was this very accurate depiction of crucifixion – a method of putting someone to death that would not be used until approximately 1,000 years in the future.

Psalm 22:17-18
> I can count all my bones. They look, they stare at me; 18 They divide my garments among them, And for my clothing they cast lots.

Jesus was crucified naked. It is somewhat difficult for us, in this age of very revealing clothing and the general acceptance of nudity, to comprehend the great humiliation Christ suffered by hanging on the Cross naked. The Roman soldiers had taken His garments and gambled for them. Jesus suffered this disgrace so that we might be clothed in His righteousness, thus enabling us to stand before God throughout eternity.

---

a. Psalm 22:15 Lit *to*
b. Psalm 22:16 Or *An assembly*; c. Another reading is *Like a lion, my...*

Psalm 22:19-20

But You, O LORD, be not far off; O You my help, hasten to my assistance. 20 Deliver my [a]soul from the sword, My only *life* from the [b]power of the dog.

Jesus cried out for God to help Him quickly; to deliver Him from the "power of the dog" – the power of the Roman soldiers.

Psalm 22:22

I will tell of Your name to my brethren; In the midst of the assembly I will praise You.

Roughly 1,000 years later, these are virtually the same words Christ repeated on the Cross. He did not die defeated. This is the Gospel – the Good News.

Later, Peter preached in the midst of the Sanhedrin. The highest Jewish council in the first century was comprised of both Pharisees (those separated to study The Law) and Sadducees (high priests).

Acts 4:12

And there is salvation in no one else; for there is no other name under heaven that has been given among men by which we must be saved."

Psalm 22:25-26

From You *comes* my praise in the great assembly; I shall pay my vows before those who fear Him. 26 The [c]afflicted will eat and be satisfied; Those who seek Him will praise the LORD. Let your heart live forever!

Christ did His part; He paid His vows. The redeemed, those who accept Him, will be in the great assembly to praise Him.

---

a. Psalm 22:20 Or *life*; b. Lit *paw*
c. Psalm 22:26 Or *poor*

Luke 23:42-43
And he was saying, "Jesus, remember me when You come [a]in Your kingdom!" 43 And He said to him, "Truly I say to you, today you shall be with Me in Paradise."

The thief, by his own admission (and by the standards of Rome) was unfit to live on earth. Even so, he believed, and as he hung on the cross next to Jesus he asked to be remembered. On that very day, the Lord Jesus made him fit for heaven – by His own death on the Cross.

Psalm 22:31
They will come and will declare His righteousness
To a people who will be born,
that He has performed it.

This includes you and me, but it will not be our righteousness, for God says that our righteousness is as filthy rags in His sight. How will His righteousness be declared? With the last word that Christ spoke on the Cross – "tetelestai" – finished, completed.

Redemption is a completed package. He has presented it to us, all wrapped up — a precious gift. You will not need to bring your do-it-yourself kit; you cannot add anything to the package. When Christ – the Perfect Sacrifice – died on the Cross, He fulfilled what was required by God. He did it all. We can do nothing but accept or reject His Gift.

This Psalm has revealed the heart of our Savior. He became a perfect sin offering on our behalf. There was no one else, and nothing else – no other sacrifice would be sufficient. Christ completed this transaction triumphantly. He offers us finished redemption. Over 2,000 years ago the Lord Jesus Christ did all that was needed to save us. And at the end, He said "finished" – period.

a. Luke 23:42 Or *into*

CHAPTER 22: THE GREAT SHEPHERD

Psalm 23 is one of the most familiar passages in the Bible. Both Orthodox and Reformed Jews, and Christians of all denominations are very well acquainted with this Psalm. The world has caught its beauty, and many people can recite it from memory. Volumes have been written about it, yet it contains only six short verses.

Even though brief, Psalm 23 is very clear and to the point – packed to overflowing with the love of our Savior. Yet, not everyone who quotes Psalm 23 truly understands its meaning. It is necessary to first understand Psalm 22, where Christ is the Good Shepherd who gave His life for the sheep, before you can know Him as the Great Shepherd of Psalm 23.

Psalm 23:1-2
A Psalm of David
> The LORD is my shepherd, I [a]shall not want.
> 2 He makes me lie down in green pastures;
> He leads me beside [b]quiet waters.

This is a "He" and "me" Psalm. The emphasis is that nothing lies between man's soul and God. The LORD "is" my shepherd. This is both a declaration and a deduction. By stating that "the LORD is my shepherd," you are claiming Him as *your* shepherd because of His redemptive work on the Cross and your acceptance of that redemptive work.

John 3:16
> "For God so loved the world, that He gave His [c]only begotten Son, that whoever believes in Him shall not perish, but have eternal life.

---

a. Psalm 23:1 Or *do*
b. Psalm 23:2 Lit *waters of rest*
c. John 3:16 Or *unique,* only one of His kind

John 3:17-18

> For God did not send the Son into the world to judge the world, but that the world might be saved through Him. 18 He who believes in Him is not judged; he who does not believe has been judged already, because he has not believed in the name of the [a]only begotten Son of God.

It is very important to realize that Psalm 23 does not apply to those who have not accepted Christ as their personal Savior.

This Psalm not only indicates the unsurpassed love of our LORD for His followers – His children, His sheep. It also indicates our willingness to trust and to follow Him unquestioningly.

Psalm 23:3-4

> He restores my soul; He guides me in the [b]paths of righteousness For His name's sake.
>
> 4 Even though I walk through the [c]valley of the shadow of death, I fear no [d]evil, for You are with me; Your rod and Your staff, they comfort me.

David, who wrote this Psalm, because of his own sin certainly knew what it meant to have his soul restored. He was that lost sheep who had gone astray, and the LORD restored his soul. As the LORD leads in the paths of righteousness, it is up to us to follow.

John 10:23

> it was winter, and Jesus was walking in the temple in the portico of Solomon.

---

a. John 3:18 Or *unique, only one of His kind*
b. Psalm 23:3 Lit *tracks*
c. Psalm 23:4 Or *valley of deep darkness*; d. Or *harm*

John 10:24-27

The Jews then gathered around Him, and were saying to Him, "How long [a]will You keep us in suspense? If You are [b]the Christ, tell us plainly." 25 Jesus answered them, "I told you, and you do not believe; the works that I do in My Father's name, these testify of Me. 26 But you do not believe because you are not of My sheep. 27 My sheep hear My voice, and I know them, and they follow Me;

In this passage from John, Jesus was speaking to the religious rulers who were His enemies. Our Great Shepherd leads us along the right path. It is our choice to follow Him.

As believers, we have comfort and courage in death. Shadrach, Meshach, and Abednego faced just such a challenge in Daniel 3:16-25, when these young men were thrown into a furnace. It was so hot, the soldiers who threw them into the furnace were killed by the escaping heat. Shadrach, Meshach, and Abednego certainly walked through the "valley of the shadow of death" as they stood up for their beliefs. Death is the supreme test of life.

Daniel 3:24-25

Then Nebuchadnezzar the king was astounded and stood up in haste; he said to his high officials, "Was it not three men we cast bound into the midst of the fire?" They replied to the king, "Certainly, O king." 25 He said, "Look! I see four men loosed *and* walking *about* in the midst of the fire [c]without harm, and the appearance of *the* fourth is like a son of *the* gods!"

Nebuchadnezzar thought that this fourth man was the son of one of the false gods he worshiped. He did not realize that this was the true Son of God. Many

---

a. John 10:24 Lit *do You lift up our soul*; b. I.e. the Messiah
c. Daniel 3:25 Lit *there is no injury in them*

prominent Bible scholars agree that the fourth man was the pre-incarnate Christ – the Angel of the LORD.

We can find no better example of men who, regardless of the outcome, stood up for their beliefs. Shadrach, Meshach, and Abednego survived their ordeal only by the grace of God – the one true God. We can know with certainty that our Shepherd is with us at all times, even at the time of death.

A shepherd carried a staff and a rod. The rod was for defense, and the staff was for direction. Our Shepherd gives us gentle reproof, and severe rebuke. His rod is for our protection, but He also has a staff for our guidance.

Psalm 23:5-6
You prepare a table before me in the presence of my enemies; You [a]have anointed my head with oil; My cup overflows. 6 [b]Surely goodness and lovingkindness will follow me all the days of my life, And I will [c]dwell in the house of the LORD [d]forever.

The LORD will provide. He has promised to be sufficient for us. He will provide what we need, both physically and spiritually. He is adequate.

Our acceptance of Christ is our anointing. At the moment we accept Christ as our Savior, the Holy Spirit comes to dwell within us – to give us insight and understanding as we pursue an education in His Word. He provides guidance, keeping us on the right path so that we will not stray to the left or the right.

Our joy is so great when we accept Christ, that our cup overflows. Yet we are completely undeserving of such joy, because of our sinful lives.

---

a. Psalm 23:5 Or *anoint*
b. Psalm 23:6 Or *Only*; c. Another reading is *return to*; d. Lit *for length of days*

We have just taken a journey through this Psalm – through the green pastures and by the still waters, through the valley of the shadow of death, to the Father's house.

John 14:2-3

> In My Father's house are many dwelling places; if it were not so, I would have told you; for I go to prepare a place for you. 3 If I go and prepare a place for you, I will come again and receive you to Myself, that where I am, *there* you may be also.

Can you say, "the LORD is my Shepherd?" If so, all the wonderful promises of this Psalm belong to you. Knowing Christ as your Savior, as you quote this Psalm, will enable you to experience the great comfort it brings.

CHAPTER 23: CHRIST AS THE CHIEF SHEPHERD

Psalm 24 portrays Christ as the Chief Shepherd, or our wonderful sovereign King. As we examine this Psalm, we notice two themes. The first theme depicts those believers who will ascend into heaven because of the righteousness of Christ (verses 1-6), and the second theme describes the coming of our glorious King to set up His Kingdom (verses 7-10).

Psalm 24:1-2
The King of Glory Entering Zion
A Psalm of David.

> The earth is the LORD'S, and [a]all it contains,
> The world, and those who dwell in it.
> 2 For He has founded it upon the seas
> And established it upon the rivers.

David speaks of the LORD as Creator. The entire earth, all the solar systems, all the universes, belong to God – not to America or any other world rulers.

God ordered the waters to be gathered to one place, and dry land appeared. Then He ordered the vegetation, and later He ordered all living creatures into existence, and created man in His image.

Genesis 1:9-11

> Then God said, "Let the waters below the heavens be gathered into one place, and let the dry land appear"; and it was so. 10 God called the dry land earth, and the gathering of the waters He called seas; and God saw that it was good. 11 Then God said, "Let the earth sprout [b]vegetation, [c]plants yielding seed, *and* fruit trees on the earth bearing fruit after [d]their kind [e]with seed in them"; and it was so.

---

a. Psalm 24:1 Lit *its fullness*
b. Genesis 1:11 Or *grass*; c. Or *herbs*; d. Lit *its*; e. Lit *in which is its seed*

This is life out of death – the Resurrection.

Psalm 24:3
> Who may ascend into the hill of the LORD?
> And who may stand in His holy place?

The next verse answers this very pertinent question.

Psalm 24:4
> He who has clean hands and a pure heart,
> Who has not lifted up his soul [a]to falsehood
> And has not sworn deceitfully.

This definitely narrows the field of who shall ascend the hill of the LORD. There has been but One Person on this earth who could perfectly fit this description – our Lord and Savior, Jesus Christ.

He represents all true believers, and in His priestly office He will bring them to the throne of grace – not because of their accomplishments, but because of Christ's sacrifice for them. The only righteousness they will have will be the righteousness of Christ.

Psalm 24:5-6
> He shall receive a blessing from the LORD
> And [b]righteousness from the God of his salvation. 6
> [c]This is the generation of those who seek Him, Who
> seek Your face—*even* Jacob. [d]*Selah.*

Picture this multitude entering Jerusalem, singing.

Psalm 24:7
> Lift up your heads, O gates,
> And be lifted up, O [e]ancient doors,
> That the King of glory may come in!

a. Psalm 24:4 Or *in vain*
b. Psalm 24:5 I.e. as vindicated
c. Psalm 24:6 Or *Such*; d. *Selah* may mean: *Pause, Crescendo* or *Musical interlude*
e. Psalm 24:7 Lit *everlasting*

In the next verse we hear a voice from the gate inquiring, "who is the King of glory?"

Psalm 24:8-9

> Who is the King of glory?
> The LORD strong and mighty,
> The LORD mighty in battle.
> 9 Lift up your heads, O gates,
> And lift *them* up, O [a]ancient doors,
> That the King of glory may come in!

And again, the voice from the gates inquires, "Who is this King of glory?" The answer came from the multitude – probably a full choir and orchestra.

Psalm 24:10

> Who is this King of glory?
> The LORD of hosts,
> He is the King of glory. *Selah.*

Two events are portrayed here. The first is when the Lord returned to Heaven, after He had fulfilled His role as the sacrificial Lamb – that Perfect Sacrifice for your sin and mine on the Cross.

The next event portrayed is His return to earth as Judge. He will return as LORD, strong and mighty in battle.

He is not in the world today. The world has rejected Him. But He is the LORD of hosts. He is the Lord Jesus Christ, King of kings and Lord of lords – the King of glory.

The Psalmist writes Selah at the conclusion of this Psalm. Selah – pay attention, pause, and consider this for a little while.

---

a. Psalm 24:9 Lit *everlasting*

CHAPTER 24: TO BE BETRAYED BY A FRIEND

Psalm 41:9
> Even my close friend in whom I trusted,
> Who ate my bread, Has lifted up his heel against me.

This prophecy concerns the ultimate example of the most despicable betrayal in the history of mankind. It was written by King David approximately 1,000 years before it was fulfilled, when Judas Iscariot betrayed the Lord Jesus Christ.

John 13:18
> I do not speak of all of you. I know the ones I have chosen; but *it is* that the Scripture may be fulfilled, 'HE WHO EATS MY BREAD HAS LIFTED UP HIS HEEL AGAINST ME.'

Jesus was speaking of Judas. Peter also referred to this terrible deed in Acts, when Judas Iscariot was identified as the betrayer.

Acts 1:16
> "Brethren, the Scripture had to be fulfilled, which the Holy Spirit foretold by the mouth of David concerning Judas, who became a guide to those who arrested Jesus.

This is yet another confirmation of fulfilled prophecy concerning Christ's sacrifice for all believers.

CHAPTER 25: THE REIGN OF GOD'S ANOINTED

Psalm 45 is a Messianic Psalm, a picture of Christ as Messiah – Bridegroom to the Church. It is a Maschil, a wedding song of love, written by the sons of Korah. The great importance of this Psalm is reiterated as several verses are quoted in the Epistle to the Hebrews.

This Psalm describes the Second Coming of Christ. It changes tenor from a cry of people in Tribulation, to the glorious triumph of their coming King, as detailed in Revelation 19. Our Lord Jesus Christ vividly draws a picture of His Second Coming in the Book of Matthew.

Matthew 24:29-30

"But immediately after the tribulation of those days THE SUN WILL BE DARKENED, AND THE MOON WILL NOT GIVE ITS LIGHT, AND THE STARS WILL FALL from [a]the sky, and the powers of [b]the heavens will be shaken. 30 And then the sign of the Son of Man will appear in the sky, and then all the tribes of the earth will mourn, and they will see the SON OF MAN COMING ON THE CLOUDS OF THE SKY with power and great glory.

Psalm 45:1
A Song Celebrating the King's Marriage.
For the choir director; according to the [c]Shoshannim. A [d]Maskil of the sons of Korah. A Song of Love.

My heart [e]overflows with a good theme;
I [f]address my [g]verses to the [h]King;
My tongue is the pen of a ready writer.

Overflowing means full of enthusiasm, bursting forth. The writer has such good news to relay he would

---

a. Matthew 24:29 Or *heaven*; b. Or *heaven*
c. Psalm 45:1 Or possibly *Lilies*; d. Possibly *Contemplative*, or *Didactic*, or *Skillful Psalm*; e. Lit *is astir*; f. Lit *am saying*; g. Lit *works*; h.Probably refers to Solomon as a type of Christ

rather say it out loud, because his tongue moves faster than his pen. That's true of many of us. Have you ever been so excited about something you wanted to put it in a letter? It is usually much easier to tell your news in person, enthusiastically, rather than write it down.

Despite our careful attention, it is easy to lose or forget something in the telling. A more reliable avenue would be to record our message in some manner, editing as we recall more details. In this present day of advanced technology, we have various and sundry methods of recording information, which are much easier and quicker than those available at the time the Psalms were written.

Psalm 45:2
You are fairer than the sons of men; Grace is poured [a]upon Your lips; Therefore God has blessed You forever.

What a beautiful verse! It describes the person of Christ. He is fairer than all humans, and is gracious in His speech. This verse in the ancient writings of the Chaldean Targum is translated, [b]"Thy beauty, O King Messiah, is greater than that of the sons of men." Paul further mentioned the glory of the Lord in his second letter to the Corinthians.

2 Corinthians 3:18
But we all, with unveiled face, beholding as in a mirror the glory of the Lord, are being transformed into the same image from glory to glory, just as from the Lord, the Spirit.

Certainly we need to look upon Him more, and as this Psalm reminds us – we should be viewing Him as Savior and King.

---

a. Psalm 45:2 Or *through*
b. Gaebelein, Arno Clemens. "Gaebelein's Annotated Bible".1913-1922.

Psalm 45:3
Gird Your sword on *Your* thigh, O [a]Mighty One,
In Your splendor and Your majesty!

This is a picture of Christ coming forward not as a Savior but as the King, at His Second Coming. Israel expected Messiah to come to earth with a sword the first time. Instead, He came to seek and to save that which was lost.

When Jesus was arrested, his disciple Peter used a sword to cut off the ear of one of the servants of the high priest.

Matthew 26:52
Then Jesus *said to him, "Put your sword back into its place; for all those who take up the sword shall perish by the sword.

Today, many people are awaiting the Messiah who will bring peace without a sword. However, a very different description is found in Psalm 2, which describes Christ coming to earth a second time. This passage is also quoted several times in the Book of Revelation.

Psalm 2:9
'You shall [b]break them with a [c]rod of iron,
You shall shatter them like [d]earthenware.'"

When Messiah returns, He will find the world in rebellion. Observe the world now. It is no wonder many people think His return is near. Still, there are a few things than must happen before He comes back to rule the earth.

---

a. Psalm 45:3 Or *warrior*
b. Psalm 2:9 Another reading is *rule*; c. Or *scepter* or *staff*; d. Lit *potter's ware*

Antichrist will be in power and will be persecuting God's people – both the remnant of Israel, and the great company of Gentiles who have turned to God. There will be condemnation and judgment. We must be realistic in our expectations. Christ will come in power and wrath against the world that is against Him.

Psalm 45:4
> And in Your majesty ride on victoriously,
> For the cause of truth and meekness *and* righteousness;
> Let Your right hand teach You [a]awesome things.

Not many of today's leaders possess these three qualities: *truth, meekness,* and *righteousness.* Only a handful sound meek. The truth doesn't seem to be found in many of them. Perhaps a very few could be considered righteous.

In contrast, when the Lord returns He will bring with him truth, humility and righteousness, and He will establish a Perfect Dictatorship.

Psalm 45:5
> Your arrows are sharp;
> The peoples fall under You;
> *Your arrows are* in the heart of the
> King's enemies.

This is certainly a portrait of the King coming to earth.

Psalm 45:6
> Your throne, O God, is forever and ever; A scepter
> of uprightness is the scepter of Your kingdom.

He will rule in righteousness. Oh, how this world needs an upright ruler!

---

a. Psalm 45:4 Or *fearful*

Matthew 25:31
> "But when the Son of Man comes in His glory, and all the angels with Him, then He will sit on His glorious throne.

His Second Coming will be as King.

Psalm 45:7
> You have loved righteousness and hated wickedness;
> Therefore God, Your God, has anointed You
> With the oil of joy above Your fellows.

The anointed one is the Messiah, the Christ. This is not a name, but His official title. As He came to us the first time, He came as a prophet. He was a messenger, and He carried the message of God.

His present-day ministry is as our great High Priest who sits at the right hand of God. When He returns, it will be as Ruler and King.

Notice that He was anointed with the oil of joy. It is odd that we tend to think of Jesus as a man of sorrows. (We'll explore more about this later.)

CHAPTER 26: GALL AND VINEGAR

Psalm 69:20-21
> Reproach has broken my heart and I am so sick.
> And I looked for sympathy, but there was none,
> And for comforters, but I found none.
> 21 They also gave me [a]gall [b]for my food
> And for my thirst they gave me vinegar to drink.

This is a very vivid picture of our Lord's dark hours on the Cross. It is recorded in three of the four gospels. Jesus is alone on the Cross with the sins of the world upon His shoulders. His Jewish people, filled with reproach, have rejected Him to the extent of insisting that He be crucified. His disciples have deserted Him, and those who love Him are being kept at a distance.

Matthew 27:34
> they gave Him wine to drink mixed with gall; and after tasting *it*, He was unwilling to drink.

Mark 15:23
> They tried to give Him wine mixed with myrrh; but He did not take it.

John 19:28-30
> After this, Jesus, knowing that all things had already been accomplished, to fulfill the Scripture, *said, "I am thirsty." 29 A jar full of sour wine was standing there; so they put a sponge full of the sour wine upon *a branch of* hyssop and brought it up to His mouth. 30 Therefore when Jesus had received the sour wine, He said, "It is finished!" And He bowed His head and gave up His spirit.

---

a. Psalm 69:21 Or *poison*; b. Or *in*

CHAPTER 27: HIS GLORIOUS REIGN

Psalm 72 is all about the Messiah establishing His glorious Kingdom on earth. Because it is prefaced, "of Solomon," some think Solomon wrote this Psalm; however, I believe it was written for Solomon by his father David.

Psalm 72:1-3
The Reign of the Righteous King
A *Psalm* of Solomon.

> Give the king Your judgments, O God,
> And Your righteousness to the king's son.
> 2 [a]May [b]he judge Your people with righteousness
> And [c]Your afflicted with justice.
> 3 [d]Let the mountains bring [e]peace to the people,
> And the hills, in righteousness.

Notice that the writer asks God to give His righteousness to the king's son.

Psalm 72:7
> In his days [f]may the righteous flourish,
> And abundance of peace till the moon is
> no more.

Righteousness is the theme throughout these verses. The Lord Jesus will rule His glorious, peaceful Kingdom in righteousness. Contrary to popular belief, there will be no lasting peace on earth until His Kingdom is established.

---

a. Psalm 72:2 Or *He* will *judge*; b. Many of the pronouns in this Psalm may be rendered *He* since the typical reference is to the Messiah; c. Or *Your humble*
d. Psalm 72:3 Or *The mountains will bring*; e. Or *prosperity*
f. Psalm 72:7 Or *the righteous will flourish*

Psalm 72:17-19

> May his name endure forever; May his name [a]increase [b]as long as the sun *shines*; And let *men* bless themselves by him; Let all nations call him blessed.
>
> 18 Blessed be the LORD God, the God of Israel, Who alone works wonders. 19 And blessed be His glorious name forever; And may the whole earth be filled with His glory. Amen, and Amen.

God gave this vision of His future Kingdom and the coming Christ to David, who prayed for the whole earth to be filled with glory of the LORD.

Psalm 72:20

> The prayers of David the son of Jesse are ended.

Verse 20 indicates that David was indeed the writer of this Psalm. David's prayers are ended – he is through praying. What David prayed for – God's Promise – he knew would be realized; he had no other prayer.

---

a. Psalm 72:17 Or *sprout forth*; b. Lit *before the sun*

CHAPTER 28: TO SPEAK IN PARABLES

In Psalm 78, we observe Jesus' favorite teaching method and the reason He taught in this manner.

Psalm 78:2
> I will open my mouth in a parable;
> I will utter dark sayings of old,

The word parable is taken from the Greek word, *parabole*. It is a type of short story used to precisely illustrate a moral truth. Using a parable is like placing a carpenter's rule onto a piece of lumber to measure the length before cutting, in order to make a precise cut.

Our Lord Jesus used parables to relate, or measure, heavenly truth. In these parables, He chose common-place objects and situations which people of that day, and even today, would be able to comprehend very well. He spoke of the weather – the wind and rain; of vegetation – fig trees, lilies, vines, corn; of birds – the sparrow and raven. His words were often those descriptive of nature; familiar words that the average person would understand. This was a very natural and enlightening method to teach those who desired to learn the truth.

Some 800-1,000 years after this Psalm was written, we observe Jesus teaching with parables.

Matthew 13:10
> And the disciples came and said to Him, "Why do You speak to them in parables?"

The disciples asked a meaningful question. Someone has appropriately likened a parable to "an earthly story with a heavenly meaning."

Matthew 13:11
> [a]Jesus answered them, "To you it has been granted to know the mysteries of the kingdom of heaven, but to them it has not been granted.

Jesus explained that His disciples (believers) have been given discernment to understand, but others – those with hardened hearts – do not desire to understand. The Bible, God's Word, to a person without the Holy Spirit – without discernment – does not make sense.

Matthew 13:12
> For whoever has, to him *more* shall be given, and he will have an abundance; but whoever does not have, even what he has shall be taken away from him.

Those who have some measure of discernment, and a desire for more, will receive an abundance of understanding. Those not interested (the hard-hearted) will lose what little understanding they possess.

Matthew 13:13
> Therefore I speak to them in parables; because while seeing they do not see, and while hearing they do not hear, nor do they understand.

This sounds a little like listening to my algebra teacher in high school. In the beginning of the class, I certainly did not understand the subject being taught. But I did listen, and try to understand.

Those who are humble and have an open heart, and who are interested, will see, hear, and gain understanding. But those who have no interest – who have hardened hearts – will fail to comprehend.

---

a. Matthew 13:11 Lit *He*

Matthew 13:14-15

[a]In their case the prophecy of Isaiah is being fulfilled, which says,

> '[b]YOU WILL KEEP ON HEARING, [c]BUT WILL NOT UNDERSTAND; [d]YOU WILL KEEP ON SEEING, BUT WILL NOT PERCEIVE; 15 FOR THE HEART OF THIS PEOPLE HAS BECOME DULL, WITH THEIR EARS THEY SCARCELY HEAR, AND THEY HAVE CLOSED THEIR EYES, OTHERWISE THEY WOULD SEE WITH THEIR EYES, HEAR WITH THEIR EARS, AND UNDERSTAND WITH THEIR HEART AND RETURN, AND I WOULD HEAL THEM.'

Isaiah 6:9

He said, "Go, and tell this people:

> 'Keep on listening, but do not perceive;
> Keep on looking, but do not understand.'

This was Isaiah's first commission. He was to go and tell the people – the nation Israel. At first glance, it appears that the prophet is being sent to the blind and deaf – the people who are hardened and not open to God's Word. We are born with hardened hearts. Shining the Light of Truth on a person simply brings their true character to the surface.

As a child growing up, I lived on a farm. Many times, especially during tobacco season, we worked late into the evening. Yet we still had to go to the barn to feed the animals and milk the cows. As I entered the barn at night and turned on the light, rats scurried for cover. They were seeking darkness because they did not like the light.

---

a. Matthew 13:14 Lit *For them*; b. Lit *With a hearing you will hear*; c. Lit *and*; d. Lit *Seeing you will see*

If the lights remained on for a while, as the chores were done, the birds who took shelter in the rafters of the barn would twitter and sing. The birds loved the light, but the rats hated it. Shining the light on the rats did not change them from being rats.

Another illustration of this principle is shown in this story about a group of miners who were trapped in pure darkness for several days after a mining explosion. When a small hole was finally opened to them by rescuers, the first things placed through the hole were an air hose and a light. After the light had been on for some time, one of the young miners who was trapped asked, "When are they going to turn on the light?" The other miners then realized that the explosion had blinded this young miner.

The blinded miner had been on equal footing with the other trapped miners while they were all in total darkness. Only when the light was turned on and he could not see was his difference noticed.

Jesus is the Light. He is Love and Life. God's Word was shining the Light, and the Light was not received.

Matthew 13:34-35
> All these things Jesus spoke to the crowds in parables, and He did not speak to them without a parable. 35 *This was* to fulfill what was spoken through the prophet:
>
> "I WILL OPEN MY MOUTH IN PARABLES;
> I WILL UTTER THINGS HIDDEN SINCE THE
> FOUNDATION OF THE WORLD."

The parables Jesus spoke reveal truths previously shrouded in mystery, but only those people who believe in Him have the gift of understanding. Jesus did not say anything to the crowds without using a parable. As He spoke in parables, Jesus was fulfilling prophecy.

CHAPTER 29: HARDENED HEARTS

Proverbs 28:14
How blessed is the man who fears always,
But he who hardens his heart will fall into calamity.

In the Word of God, the term *hardened hearts* describes unbelievers, skeptics, the rebellious and disobedient. One of the best examples of this is found in Exodus.

Exodus 7:2-3
You shall speak all that I command you, and your brother Aaron shall speak to Pharaoh that he let the sons of Israel go out of his land. 3 But I will harden Pharaoh's heart that I may multiply My signs and My wonders in the land of Egypt.

This appears to say that God would harden Pharaoh's heart. Did God actually harden Pharaoh's heart? In a way, yes. Pharaoh's nature was not that of a sweet, tenderhearted guy who desired to turn to God and happily see the children of Israel leave Egypt because he wanted to do something good for them.

God hardened Pharaoh's heart by revealing his true nature. We've all heard the term, "the buck stops here." Well, the buck stopped with Pharaoh – the ruler to whom Moses was sent to ask for the children of Israel to be released from Egyptian slavery.

Man is unlike any of the other creations of God, in that God created man in His own image – with a free will. Man can make up his mind to do whatever his nature leads him to do. This is true with all of us. We can decide to do good, or to do evil. God could have made us like robots, but He chose to give us a free will. Of course, He wants us to love Him; however, the choice is ours. Unfortunately, some choose to be a wayward lover and love things other than God.

Everyone makes an occasional wrong decision, but for some people the majority of the decisions they make are wrong. They turn a deaf ear to anything that goes against their own desires. They have hardened hearts.

CHAPTER 30: THE ENDLESSNESS OF DAVID'S THRONE

Psalm 89 is often referred to as the "Psalm of the Davidic Covenant." Written by Ethan the Ezrahite, a singer who possibly belonged to the tribe of Levi, it is a Maschil – a psalm of wisdom and instruction. The main theme, the faithfulness of God, is exalted in this psalm.

The importance of themes is reflected in the repetition of terms. God's faithfulness is mentioned ten times, and covenant is mentioned four times. God says "I have sworn" three times, and, "I will not lie" four times.

Earlier as we studied 2 Samuel, Chapter 7, which is a record of the importance of God's covenant with David, we saw the Promise emphasized again and again. This psalm is devoted to that Promise.

Psalm 89:1
The Lord's Covenant with David, and Israel's Afflictions.
A [a]Maskil of [b]Ethan [c]the Ezrahite.

> I will sing of the lovingkindness of the LORD forever;
> To all generations I will make known Your faithfulness
> with my mouth.

The Lord has given us yet another way to make known His faithfulness to all generations – with song. Notice the pronoun here is "Your." This is praise to God for His faithfulness to David and to His people. Later, in verse 24, the pronoun changes to "My," because God directly speaks at that point. Nevertheless, all of the references in this Psalm, regardless of the pronoun used, refer to the faithfulness of God.

---

a. Psalm 89:1 Possibly, *Contemplative*, or *Didactic*, or *Skillful Psalm*; b. 1 Kin 4:31; c. Ps 88: title

Psalm 89:2
> For I have said, "Lovingkindness will be built up
> forever; In the heavens You will establish Your
> faithfulness."

God is faithful. Nothing can deter His faithfulness. Our salvation depends upon the death and resurrection of Christ, and the faithfulness of God in saving those who place their trust in His saving grace. Men may change what they say, and what they promise, but God can never do this. He is always faithful to do what He says He will do. His Covenant, or Promise, is absolute.

Psalm 89:3
> "I have made a covenant with My chosen;
> I have sworn to David My servant,

God has made a covenant with David.

Psalm 89:5
> The heavens will praise Your wonders, O Lord; Your
> faithfulness also in the assembly of the holy ones.

We know the heavens declare the glory of God. We only have to open our eyes to view the wonders of the heavens and the earth. Even man's attempts to "uglify" the face of the earth cannot totally hide the beauty and splendor. God's handiwork still shows through. And the faithfulness of God has even more glory connected with it than does His marvelous creation! His great faithfulness towards us deserves our high praise.

Psalm 89:8
> O Lord God of hosts, who is like You, O mighty
> [a]Lord? Your faithfulness also surrounds You.

---

a. Psalm 89:8 Heb *Yah*

God is the mightiest of the mighty. We are assured of His unending faithfulness.

Psalm 89:20
"I have found David My servant; With My holy oil I have anointed him,

This is further affirmation that the Davidic Covenant, the Promise God made to David at his anointing, would be fulfilled.

Psalm 89:24
"My faithfulness and My lovingkindness will be with him, And in My name his horn will be exalted.

The horn speaks of the power of Christ. His power is unlimited. He sits above the circle of the earth, at the right hand of God, awaiting that day when He will make His glorious appearance.

Psalm 89:27
"I also shall make him *My* firstborn, The highest of the kings of the earth.

This is another promise to David; to send One in his line. This covenant centers on the Lord Jesus Christ – He is higher than all the kings of the earth. He is Lord of lords and King of kings.

How wonderful! God sent Jesus into this world as His only begotten Son. The Son of God, who was born of a virgin in a stable at Bethlehem, was revealed to us in a life of humiliation.

Even so, this "first born" reference is not about Jesus being born as a child in Bethlehem. Here God is speaking of the resurrected Christ. He came in resurrection – the first born, the first begotten – from the dead.

1 John 1:1-3

What was from the beginning, what we have heard, what we have seen with our eyes, what we have looked at and touched with our hands, concerning the Word of Life— 2 and the life was manifested, and we have seen and testify and proclaim to you the eternal life, which was with the Father and was manifested to us— 3 what we have seen and heard we proclaim to you also, so that you too may have fellowship with us; and indeed our fellowship is with the Father, and with His Son Jesus Christ.

Proverbs 8:22-23

"The LORD possessed me at the beginning of His way,
Before His works [a]of old.
23 "From everlasting I was [b]established,
From the beginning, from the earliest
times of the earth.

Psalm 89:28

"My lovingkindness I will keep for him forever, And
My covenant shall be confirmed to him.

Psalm 89:34-36

"My covenant I will not [c]violate,
Nor will I alter [d]the utterance of My lips.
35 "[e]Once I have sworn by My holiness;
I will not lie to David.
36 "His [f]descendants shall endure forever
And his throne as the sun before Me.

God took His Promise so seriously, that He swore an oath concerning the covenant He made with David.

---

a. Proverbs 8:22 Lit *from then*
b. Proverbs 8:23 Or *consecrated*
c. Psalm 89:34 Lit *profane*; d. Lit *that which goes forth*
e. Psalm 89:35 Or *One thing*
f. Psalm 89:36 Lit *seed*

Now, at this very moment, there is One sitting at the right hand of God. He is none other than our Lord Jesus Christ, the Son of David. One day He will return to establish His Millennial Kingdom.

Psalm 89:37
> "It shall be established forever like the moon, And the witness in the sky is faithful." [a]*Selah.*

This again confirms that David will have a Son who will sit on the Throne of this universe. This fact is established just as certainly as the moon is established in the heavens.

Psalm 89:49
> Where are Your former lovingkindnesses,
> O Lord, Which You swore to David in Your faithfulness?

When is all this going to take place? To some, it looks as if God has forgotten His covenant. God has not forgotten. He is faithful, and in His own timing His Promise will be fulfilled.

---

a. Psalm 89:37 *Selah* may mean: *Pause, Crescendo* or *Musical interlude*

CHAPTER 31: MESSIAH TO BE KING AND PRIEST

Psalm 110 is all about the exaltation of Christ. A Messianic Psalm, it begins with the ascension of Christ.

Psalm 110:1
A Psalm of David.

> The LORD says to my Lord: "Sit at My right hand
> Until I make Your enemies a footstool for Your feet."

This Psalm clearly sets forth the deity of Christ, and is referred to many times in the New Testament. (Acts 2:34-35; Hebrews 1:13, 5:6, 6:20, 7:20, 7:21, 10:12-13.) No one can consider this Psalm and still deny His deity.

The enemies of Jesus tried to trap Him into making a political statement that would mark Him as a traitor to Rome. Thus Rome would do their dirty work. When this plan failed, the Herodians took over, and then the Sadducees. These liberal religious parties tried to ensnare Christ the same way, using Mosaic Law. When they failed, the religiopolitical party, the Sanhedrin, attempted to trap Him. But His answers befuddled even this group. As they gathered to plan further strategy, Jesus posed a question.

Matthew 22:41-44
> Now while the Pharisees were gathered together, Jesus asked them a question: 42 "What do you think about [a]the Christ, whose son is He?" They *said to Him, "*The son* of David." 43 He *said to them, "Then how does David [b]in the Spirit call Him 'Lord,' saying,
>
> > 44 'THE LORD SAID TO MY LORD, "SIT AT MY RIGHT HAND,
> > UNTIL I PUT YOUR ENEMIES BENEATH YOUR FEET"'?

---

a. Matthew 22:42 I.e. the Messiah
b. Matthew 22:43 Or *by inspiration*

Matthew 22:45-46

> 45 If David then calls Him 'Lord,' how is He his son?" 46 No one was able to answer Him a word, nor did anyone dare from that day on to ask Him [a]another question.

This was a very straightforward question. When the Pharisees answered that the Christ was the *son* of David, the Lord referred them to Psalm 110. Their insufficient knowledge and understanding of that portion of Scripture caused the Jews to misinterpret this prophecy.

Psalm 110, written by David, depicts Jehovah speaking to Messiah. A Jewish person who read Psalm 110 would be faced with a decision – whether or not Messiah was David's descendant. In this Psalm, David calls Messiah his Lord; more than merely a king and political ruler on a throne.

Also, since David called Him Lord in this Psalm, how could He be his son? The Lord could not be his Son by natural birth; it had to be by supernatural birth, and this Psalm again confirms that the Lord Jesus Christ, Israel's Messiah, was virgin-born.

Psalm 110:2

> The LORD will stretch forth Your strong scepter from Zion, *saying*, "Rule in the midst of Your enemies."

Christ will come to the earth to rule.

---

a. Matthew 22:46 Lit *any longer*

Isaiah 2:3

And many peoples will come and say,
"Come, let us go up to the mountain of the LORD,
To the house of the God of Jacob; That He may
teach us [a]concerning His ways And that we may walk
in His paths." For the [b]law will go forth from Zion
And the word of the LORD from Jerusalem.

Jerusalem will be the center of the earthly government. God does have a very specific purpose for Israel in the future.

Psalm 110:3

Your people [c]will volunteer freely in the day of Your
[d]power; In [e]holy array, from the womb of the
dawn, [f]Your youth are to You *as* the dew.

During this day of power, there will be a great turning to Jesus Christ, such as the world has never seen. No, it certainly does not appear that way now – but things will change. God has the divine ability to cause that change. As we look at the world today, it is easy to be discouraged about the Church and its direction; however, this Psalm says things won't always remain this way. We can look forward in anticipation of this great revival. Perhaps it will occur in our lifetime, or perhaps during that of our descendants.

Psalm 110:4

The LORD has sworn and will not [g]change His mind,
"You are a priest forever According to the order
of Melchizedek."

---

a. Isaiah 2:3 Or *some of*; b. Or *instruction*
c. Psalm 110:3 Lit *will be freewill offerings*; d. Or *army*;
e. Or *the splendor of holiness*; f. Or *The dew of Your youth is Yours*
g. Psalm 110:4 Lit *be sorry*

This is another very important truth. The Lord Jesus is a High Priest after the order of Melchizedek. This statement is further developed in the Book of Hebrews. It is one of the greatest truths in the Word of God.

Hebrews 5:6-10

just as He says also in another *passage*,

"YOU ARE A PRIEST FOREVER
ACCORDING TO THE ORDER OF MELCHIZEDEK."

7 [a]In the days of His flesh, [b]He offered up both prayers and supplications with loud crying and tears to the One able to save Him [c]from death, and He [d]was heard because of His piety. 8 Although He was a Son, He learned obedience from the things which He suffered. 9 And having been made perfect, He became to all those who obey Him the source of eternal salvation, 10 being designated by God as a high priest according to the order of Melchizedek.

The priesthood of our Lord Jesus is superior to the Aaronic or Levitical priesthoods of the Old Testament. These verses demonstrate both the deity and the humanity of the Lord Jesus Christ.

Psalm 110:5-6

The Lord is at Your right hand; He [e]will shatter kings in the day of His wrath. 6 He will judge among the nations, He [f]will fill *them* with corpses, He [g]will shatter the [h]chief men over a broad country.

The next coming of Christ will be in judgment.

---

a. Hebrews 5:7 I.e. during Christ's earthly life; b. Lit *who having offered up*;
c. Or *out of*; d. Lit *having been heard*
e. Psalm 110:5 Or *has shattered*
f. Psalm 110:6 Or *has filled*; g. Or *has shattered*; h. Lit *head over*

Psalm 2:9

'You shall [a]break them with a [b]rod of iron, You shall shatter them like [c]earthenware.'"

Psalm 110:7

He will drink from the brook by the wayside;
Therefore He will lift up *His* head.

This again portrays both the humiliation and exaltation of our Lord. In humiliation, He drank from the brook by the wayside. Remember the 300 warriors of Gideon who on their knees, lapped water like dogs?

Judges 7:6-7

Now the number of those who lapped, putting their hand to their mouth, was 300 men; but all the rest of the people kneeled to drink water. 7 The Lord said to Gideon, "I will deliver you with the 300 men who lapped and will give the Midianites into your hands; so let all the other people go, each man to his [d]home."

They later were exalted, through victory over a much larger force, on the battlefield. Our Lord Jesus' humiliation went much deeper than that. He drank the deep waters of suffering and death; therefore, God has highly exalted Him.

---

a. Psalm 2:9 Another reading is *rule*; b. Or *scepter* or *staff*; c. Lit *potter's ware*
d. Judges 7:7 Lit *place*

CHAPTER 32: MESSIAH TO BE REJECTED BY RULERS

Psalm 118:22
> The stone which the builders rejected
> Has become the chief corner *stone*.

This *stone* refers to the Lord Jesus. Our Lord made that clear in the following verse.

Matthew 21:42
> Jesus *said to them, "Did you never read in the Scriptures,
>
> 'THE STONE WHICH THE BUILDERS REJECTED,
> THIS BECAME THE CHIEF CORNER *stone*;
> THIS CAME ABOUT FROM THE LORD,
> AND IT IS MARVELOUS IN OUR EYES'?

A cornerstone is the basic part of a building. It is the most important piece of the foundation. Without a properly installed cornerstone, the entire project would be compromised.

This is the same cornerstone mentioned in Isaiah 28:16, and in Daniel 2:45, which we will see later in this study. The stone described in these ancient writings is the Lord Jesus Christ, the solid foundation upon which we base our faith. This is a permanent foundation – it will not be moved.

CHAPTER 33: WISDOM PERSONIFIED IN CHRIST

Proverbs 8:22
> "The LORD possessed me at the beginning of His way,
> Before His works [a]of old.

This verse indicates that Jesus was with God from the beginning.

Proverbs 8:23
> "From everlasting I was [b]established, From the beginning, from the earliest times of the earth.

Some other translations say, "I was appointed from everlasting." He is the One who is the subject of John's prologue.

John 1:1-2
> In the beginning was the Word, and the Word was with God, and the Word was God. 2 [c]He was in the beginning with God.

He was begotten, not in the sense of having a beginning of life, but as being One in nature and substance with the Father. In eternity, He was God, and He was in the beginning with God. He was in the beginning *that has no beginning*, because in the beginning *was* the Word. He was already past tense at the time of the beginning.

---

a. Proverbs 8:22 Lit *from then*
b. Proverbs 8:23 Or *consecrated*
c. John 1:2 Lit *This one*

Proverbs 8:24-27

"When there were no depths I was [a]brought forth,
When there were no springs abounding with water.
"Before the mountains were settled, Before the hills
I was [b]brought forth; 26 While He had not yet made
the earth and the [c]fields, Nor the first dust of the
world. 27 "When He established the heavens, I was
there, When He inscribed a circle on the face of the
deep,

John 1:3

All things came into being through Him, and apart from
Him nothing came into being that has come into being.

It is interesting that scientists once spoke of a
square universe, but God has always said it was a circle.
You and I live in a world that is round, that travels
'round in its orbit within our planetary system. We
belong to a circular galactic system. All of these circles
are continuously rotating in such a precise manner that
nothing ever gets out of sync. We use the sun, moon,
and stars as signs to mark seasons and time in a precise
manner.

Proverbs 8:28-29

When He made firm the skies above, When the
springs of the deep became [d]fixed,
29 When He set for the sea its boundary
So that the water would not transgress His
[e]command, When He marked out the foundations
of the earth;

You can probably remember a time when you stood
by the seashore and wondered why the water didn't

---

a. Proverbs 8:24 Or *born*
b. Proverbs 8:25 Or *born*
c. Proverbs 8:26 Lit *outside places*
d. Proverbs 8:28 Lit *strong*
e. Proverbs 8:29 Lit *mouth*

spill out. Except in times of storms, it certainly does not run over. Why does the water stay where it is? This Scripture says He set a limit. God created a law – a limit – which keeps the sea in place. The tides change, but the water does not encroach beyond certain boundaries.

Proverbs 8:30-31
> Then I was beside Him, *as* a master workman;
> And I was daily *His* delight, [a]Rejoicing always before Him, 31 [b]Rejoicing in the world, His earth, And *having* my delight in the sons of men.

All things were made by the LORD. He is the Firstborn of all creation. He is superior to all. Why is this? Because, by Him, the Father brought all things into being.

Proverbs 8:32-33
> "Now therefore, O sons, listen to me, For blessed are they who keep my ways. 33 "Heed instruction and be wise, And do not neglect *it*.

We are encouraged to take heed of the LORD'S instruction; not ignore it and live as if God doesn't exist.

Proverbs 8:34-35
> "Blessed is the man who listens to me,
> Watching daily at my gates,
> Waiting at my doorposts.
> 35 "For he who finds me finds life
> And obtains favor from the LORD.

Christ is the *Door* – the Way, the Truth, and the Life. He is the only way to God. If you have Christ, you have life.

---

a. Proverbs 8:30 Or *Playing*
b. Proverbs 8:31 Or *Playing*

John 10:9
> I am the door; if anyone enters through Me,
> he will be saved, and will go in and out and
> find pasture.

Proverbs 8:36
> "But he who [a]sins against me injures himself;
> All those who hate me love death."

If you hate Christ, you love death. You are either for Him, or against Him. There is no middle ground.

---

a. Proverbs 8:36 Or *misses me*

CHAPTER 34: A MAGNIFICENT VISION OF THE MESSIANIC AGE

Our next several chapters examine the Books of Prophecy. The requirements of a prophet were very specific, as we will see in the following few pages.

The primary distinction between the major and minor prophets is the length of their writings. Regardless of their scale, the books of the minor prophets certainly imparted very important messages. We should count them all in the major leagues.

Prophets were judged on their accuracy. In order to have any credibility, a prophet had to predict local matters – events that would occur in the short-term, in addition to those that were to happen far in the future. Otherwise, the seer quite possibly would not be alive when these distant future predictions came to pass. The prophets were judged based on whether or not their short-term prophecies were accurately fulfilled.

Accurate foresight gave the prophesier validity. If an event did not transpire exactly as the prophet predicted, he was labeled a false prophet and treated as such. It was a very serious thing to be labeled a false prophet – a matter of life or death. Certainly the message of a false prophet is not in the library of inspired Scripture.

Qualifications for prophetic office, king and priest, according to the Mosaic Code, were stringent.

Deuteronomy 18:20-21

But the prophet who speaks a word presumptuously in My name which I have not commanded him to speak, or which he speaks in the name of other gods, [a]that prophet shall die.' 21 [b]You may say in your heart, 'How will we know the word which the LORD has not spoken?'

---

a. Deuteronomy 18:20 Lit *and that*
b. Deuteronomy 18:21 Lit *if you say*

> 22 When a prophet speaks in the name of the LORD, if the thing does not come about or come true, that is the thing which the LORD has not spoken. The prophet has spoken it presumptuously; you shall not be afraid of him.

What tough guidelines for the prophets!

Reviewing Isaiah's prophecies, we see those that have clearly been fulfilled. They prove that God's Word, imparted through His prophets, is infallible. Without God's inspired Word, we certainly cannot predict the future. Yet people attempt to do so all the time.

A good example of this is seen in a weather forecaster – a meteorologist. How many times have you heard a weather report predicting clear skies, and it ended up raining? Or that the temperature would reach a certain degree on a specific day, when it actually missed the mark by a wide margin?

Weather predictors have a great deal more information to work with than in the past, yet they are still not completely accurate. For instance, consider the statement, "There is a 50% chance of rain tomorrow." With this prediction, there is a 50% chance of being right. Obviously it will either rain or it won't, but if the prediction also includes, "The rain will start at 7:00 a.m.," the odds shrink to only a 25% chance of being correct. If, in addition, it is predicted that the rain will end by 5:00 p.m., there is just a 12½% chance of accuracy.

As more variables are added, accuracy becomes inversely proportional. The chance of being right becomes less and less. The weather forecast becomes just an educated guess, even with all the instrumentation and technology used today. So in a way, the weather person is a prophet (though not a biblical one).

Isaiah is often called the "Messianic Prophet" because his book imparts a magnificent vision of the coming Messiah. It is a lengthy book, so we will attempt to identify the relative passages for this study. (As we proceed with this study, please note that some verses will be overlooked, but the goal is to cover those relevant to fulfilled and not-yet-fulfilled prophecy.)

Isaiah is the first of the major prophets in the Bible. This doesn't mean that prophecy began with Isaiah, because prophetic passages occur throughout the Bible, beginning as far back as the Pentateuch – the first five books of the Bible. There are several prophetic passages in Genesis, Exodus, Leviticus, Numbers, Deuteronomy, Ruth, 1 & 2 Samuel, 1 & 2 Kings – but these books did not specifically pertain to prophecy.

The "Books of Prophecy" begin with Isaiah and continue through the Old Testament. This includes the major prophets, Isaiah, Jeremiah, Ezekiel, and Daniel, as well as the 12 minor prophets. The Books of Prophecy also contain history, poetry, and law, but their primary messages concern future events. Each writer, from Isaiah to Malachi, is a prophet of God.

The specific objective for this portion of our study is to explore prophecies pertaining particularly to the coming of Christ to the world. As we look at the time frame during which these prophecies were presented, we discover that some were forecasted thousands of years, and some hundreds of years before Christ was born in that stable in Bethlehem. Still, they all, as they relate to His First Coming, have been fulfilled.

Isaiah contains more prophecies regarding the coming of Christ than any other portion of the Bible. (Psalms is second.)

Chapters 2-5 of Isaiah deal with the Great Tribulation period and the future Kingdom on earth.

Isaiah 2:2
> Now it will come about that In the last days
> The mountain of the house of the LORD
> Will be established [a]as the chief of the mountains,
> And will be raised above the hills; And all the nations
> will stream to it.

This is not about the last days of the Church (the time of spiritual apostasy – abandonment). Paul makes this clear in his Epistles to Timothy. The latter times of the Church and the last days of Israel are not identical, and they are not contemporary – they simply do not cover the same period of time.

In this verse, "the last days" refers to the Great Tribulation. Jesus made this clear when His disciples questioned Him, "When will these things happen?" Luke 21 refers to the destruction of Jerusalem during the last days. The Great Tribulation ends with the Second Coming of Christ when He establishes His Kingdom.

The word "mountain" in Scripture refers to a kingdom, authority, or rule. The LORD'S house is above all kingdoms on earth. After the Tribulation, the Lord Jesus will be King of kings and Lord of lords, over all the kingdoms of the world. This is clarified by Daniel.

Daniel 2:35
> Then the iron, the clay, the bronze, the silver and the gold were crushed [b]all at the same time and became like chaff from the summer threshing floors; and the wind carried them away so that not a trace of them was found. But the stone that struck the statue became a great mountain and filled the whole earth.

---

a. Isaiah 2:2 Lit *on*
b. Daniel 2:35 Lit *like one*

Isaiah 2:3

> And many peoples will come and say,
> "Come, let us go up to the mountain of the Lord,
> To the house of the God of Jacob;
> That He may teach us [a]concerning His ways
> And that we may walk in His paths."
> For the [b]law will go forth from Zion
> And the word of the LORD from Jerusalem.

Both government and religion must center in Jerusalem, and the Lord Jesus will be the Absolute Ruler. He will sit on the Throne of David. The main concern of the earth's inhabitants during the Millennial Kingdom will be to discover and do the will of God.

Isaiah 2:4

> And He will judge between the nations,
> And will [c]render decisions for many peoples;
> And they will hammer their swords into plowshares
> and their spears into pruning hooks. Nation will not
> lift up sword against nation, And never again will
> they learn war.

This will occur during the millennium, or the thousand-year rule, when Jesus governs the earth. It will be the Perfect Kingdom – an absolute monarchy. He will not need a Congress, Senate, or any other government entity.

In Joel we see just the opposite of beating swords into plowshares – beating plowshares into swords.

Joel 3:10

> Beat your plowshares into swords
> And your pruning hooks into spears;
> Let the weak say, "I am a mighty man."

---

a. Isaiah 2:3 Or *some of*; b. Or *instruction*
c. Isaiah 2:4 Or *reprove many*

Terrorist attacks which have caused the deaths of thousands of Americans are certainly examples of this activity. Today nearly every country, particularly in the Middle East, is armed to the teeth, and none trust their neighbors.

During the thousand-year rule, all people will live together in harmony and peace – a peace which will be brought about only by the rule of the Lord Jesus Christ.

Isaiah 4:2
> In that day the Branch of the LORD will be beautiful and glorious, and the fruit of the earth *will be* the pride and the adornment of the survivors of Israel.

The phrase "in that day" refers to the day of the LORD. It is repeated again and again in Isaiah and other prophetic books of the Bible. It is also mentioned in the New Testament. Joel describes that day in detail.

Joel 3:14-17
> Multitudes, multitudes in the valley of [a]decision!
> For the day of the LORD is near in the valley of [b]decision. 15 The sun and moon grow dark
> And the stars lose their brightness.
> 16 The LORD roars from Zion
> And utters His voice from Jerusalem,
> And the heavens and the earth tremble.
> But the LORD is a refuge for His people
> And a stronghold to the sons of Israel.
> 17 Then you will know that I am the LORD
> your God, Dwelling in Zion, My holy mountain.
> So Jerusalem will be holy,
> And strangers will pass through it no more.

---

a. Joel 3:14 I.e. God's verdict; b. I.e. God's verdict

Joel 3:18
Judah Will Be Blessed

> 18 And in that day
> The mountains will drip with [a]sweet wine,
> And the hills will flow with milk,
> And all the brooks of Judah will flow with water;
> And a spring will go out from the house of the LORD
> To water the valley of [b]Shittim.

It begins as every Hebrew day begins – at sundown. It begins with darkness and moves forward to the dawn. It begins with the Great Tribulation and continues into the Millennial Kingdom.

Isaiah 4:2 also contains a reference to the Lord Jesus Christ, for He is "the Branch." There are 18 Hebrew words translated as the one English word "Branch," and all of them refer to the Lord Jesus. In this particular verse, the word Branch means sprout. We will later see that He is the Branch out of dry ground; He is something green which has sprouted in the desert.

Isaiah 4:5

> then the LORD will create over the whole area of Mount Zion and over her assemblies a cloud by day, even smoke, and the brightness of a flaming fire by night; for over all the glory will be a canopy.

The glory of God will be upon every house in the Kingdom, not just upon the temple. God's glory will be complete and visible. It will be a shelter over His Kingdom. What a great and glorious day that will be!

---

a. Joel 3:18 Lit *freshly pressed out grape juice*; b. Or *acacias*

Isaiah 4:6

There will be a shelter to *give* shade from the heat by day, and refuge and [a]protection from the storm and the rain.

Many believe that when Israel was declared a nation and returned to their land in 1948, to some extent prophecy was fulfilled. But according to Scripture, when this prophecy is fulfilled there will be peace. Today there is no peace in Israel. We hear daily reports of multiple killings of both Israelis and Palestinians.

Today Israel is a sensitive piece of real estate, because it is the very spot God has chosen to be the political and religious center of the world during the Kingdom Age. With the current volatile situation in the Middle East, Israel is like a bomb with the fuse burning.

When this prophecy is fulfilled, the Lord Jesus Christ will be in charge. There will be no more unrest, no more suicide bombers, no more war. God's chosen people will be returned to their land. God gave them the land centuries ago, in the days of Abraham. This will completely fulfill God's promise to Abraham.

Peace always follows grace, mercy and cleansing. The problem has never been with a political party. It has never been with a foreign country. The problem is within the human heart. Man is a war-like creature, and he refuses to deal with his shortcomings. One war will follow another, regardless of who tries to arrange peace, until the heart of man is changed.

Isaiah 7:13

Then he said, "Listen now, O house of David! Is it too slight a thing for you to try the patience of men, that you will try the patience of my God as well?

---

a. Isaiah 4:6 Lit *a hiding place*

Facing war with Syria and Israel, King Ahaz had been advised by God to ask for a sign to bolster his faith, but Ahaz refused. Despite his refusal, the Lord gave Ahaz a sign. In fact, it was a sign for the entire house of David.

Isaiah 7:14

Therefore the Lord Himself will give you a sign: Behold, a [a]virgin will be with child and bear a son, and she will call His name [b]Immanuel.

This verse foretells Christ (Immanuel) being born of Mary. It is corroborated – historically confirmed – in all four gospels. Yet, instead of the evidence, some people choose not to believe in the virgin birth; they think it is impossible – that miracles are impossible.

In these very prophecies we are reviewing – found all through the Old Testament – from Genesis to Malachi, the birth of Christ is foretold over and over again. The inspired Word of God makes it very real.

Let's look again at Isaiah's revelation. Isaiah said that His name would be "Immanuel." But you cannot find any place in the gospels where He is called by that name. Immanuel means "God with us." He was called Jesus, because He would save His people from their sins. However, He cannot save the people from their sins unless He is Immanuel, God with us. Every time you call Him Jesus, you are saying "God with us." He is God. He is God with us, and God for us. He is our Savior, born of a virgin.

---

a. Isaiah 7:14 Or *maiden*; b. I.e. God is with us

CHAPTER 35: THE WONDERFUL CHILD

The theme in this chapter is the prophecy of the child ascending to David's throne. It is about the dark days attending His First Coming and preceding His Second Coming.

Isaiah 9:1

[a]But there will be no *more* gloom for her who was in anguish; in earlier times He treated the land of Zebulun and the land of Naphtali with contempt, but later on He shall make *it* glorious, by the way of the sea, on the other side of Jordan, Galilee of the [b]Gentiles.

This verse pertains to the Syrian invasions of the northern kingdom (Israel). The first invasion occurred when Israel was under the rule of King Menahem.

2 Kings 15:19-20

Pul, king of Assyria, came against the land, and Menahem gave Pul a thousand talents of silver so that his hand might be with him to strengthen the kingdom [c]under his rule. 20 Then Menahem exacted the money from Israel, even from all the mighty men of wealth, from each man fifty shekels of silver to pay the king of Assyria. So the king of Assyria returned and did not remain there in the land.

The Syrians were paid one thousand talents of silver – 37½ tons! They received their payment and departed.

In the second invasion, during the reign of King Pekah of Israel, the Israelites were taken captive and deported to Assyria.

---

a. Isaiah 9:1 Ch 8:23 in Heb; b. Or *nations*
c. 2 Kings 15:19 Lit *in his hand*

2 Kings 15:29
> In the days of Pekah king of Israel, [a]Tiglath-pileser
> king of Assyria came and [b]captured Ijon and
> Abel-beth-maacah and Janoah and Kedesh and Hazor
> and Gilead and Galilee, all the land of Naphtali;
> and he carried them captive to Assyria.

Jesus was neither born nor raised in Jerusalem.
Nazareth was His hometown. When Nazareth rejected
Him, He moved to Capernaum, on the Sea of Galilee, in
the despised periphery of the kingdom (Israel).

Luke 4:24
> And He said, "Truly I say to you, no prophet is
> welcome in his hometown.

Zebulun and Naphtali were located in the north.
Naphtali was on the west bank of the Sea of Galilee, and
Zebulun bordered Naphtali on the west.

Isaiah 9:2
> [c]The people who walk in darkness
> Will see a great light; Those who live in a dark
> land, The light will shine on them.

Regardless of how we translate verse one, it is clear
the people who lived in the despised Galilee were in the
darkness of paganism and religious tradition. Mosaic
Law, Judaism, and paganism were intermingled. When
our Lord began His ministry in that area, the people
saw a Great Light. They saw the Light of the Lord Jesus,
the Light of life, the Light of the world.

Psalm 36:9
> For with You is the fountain of life;
> In Your light we see light.

---

a. 2 Kings 15:29 In 1 Chr 5:6, 26, *Tilgath-pilneser*; b. Lit *took*
c. Isaiah 9:2 Ch 9:1 in Heb

John 8:12
Jesus Is the Light of the World

> Then Jesus again spoke to them, saying, "I am the Light of the world; he who follows Me will not walk in the darkness, but will have the Light of life."

Isaiah's prophecy is fulfilled.

Isaiah 9:6-7

> For a child will be born to us, a son will be given to us; And the government will [a]rest on His shoulders; And His name will be called Wonderful Counselor, Mighty God, Eternal Father, Prince of Peace. 7 There will be no end to the increase of *His* government or of peace, On the throne of David and over his kingdom, To establish it and to uphold it with justice and righteousness From then on and forevermore. The zeal of the LORD of hosts will accomplish this.

How is this going to happen? This is not a reference to the First Coming of Christ. Some Christians seem to think it is, because they quote it at Christmas.

Actually, this passage refers to the Second Coming of Christ. Notice the statement, "the government will rest on His shoulders." This has not yet happened. Christians call His name Wonderful – others do not. As Christians, we know He is the Mighty God, the Eternal Father, and the Prince of Peace. It is heartbreaking that all people do not realize this truth.

In verse seven, we see that there will be no end to the peace which He brings, and that His Kingdom will be ordered – established and upheld with justice and righteousness – forever. This has not yet occurred. This passage is definitely a reference to His Second Coming.

---

a. Isaiah 9:6 Lit *be*

Notice the descriptive names that are attributed to our Lord. His first one – Wonderful. This is not an adjective. This is His name. In Joshua 5:14 the pre-incarnate Christ appears as the captain of the host of the LORD.

Judges 13:18
But the angel of the Lord said to him, "Why do you ask my name, seeing it is [a]wonderful?"

In this verse, the same word is used.

Matthew 11:27
All things have been handed over to Me by My Father; and no one knows the Son except the Father; nor does anyone know the Father except the Son, and anyone to whom the Son wills to reveal *Him*.

The people of His time did not recognize it, but He *is* Wonderful. Still today, people do not see this. Even Christians – those who have trusted Him as their Savior – do not realize how truly Wonderful He is! Our limited knowledge and capacity for understanding does not allow us to fully grasp this truth.

Another of His names, the Mighty God – El Gibbor in Hebrew, describes the One to whom all power is given. He is the omnipotent, all powerful, almighty, divine God. He is no longer that tiny baby lying helpless in Mary's arms.

Eternal Father means Father of Eternity or Ever-lasting Father. He is the Creator of all things, all time, all ages, and has control of the purpose of all things.

John 1:3
All things came into being through Him, and apart from Him nothing came into being that has come into being.

---

a. Judges 13:18 I.e. incomprehensible

CHAPTER 36: THE REIGN OF THE BRANCH

All about the person and the power of the King, and also the purpose and the program of the Kingdom, this is continuing prophecy which began in Chapter 7 of Isaiah. Taking place during the reign of King Ahaz, Chapter 11 is one of the great Messianic prophecies of Scripture. It is about Christ coming to establish His Kingdom, and the type of rule He will impart.

Isaiah 11:1
> Then a shoot will spring from the stem of Jesse,
> And a branch from his roots will bear fruit.

In Isaiah 4:2 we saw the Branch of the LORD, mentioned again here. Notice the shoot will come from the stem of Jesse. King David is not mentioned. The one who is mentioned is David's father, Jesse. We know that Jesus was born to the young virgin, Mary, in the line of David. Why does Isaiah specifically mention Jesse, when the royal line began with David?

Jesse was a farmer and sheepherder who lived in a little out-of-the-way place called Bethlehem. By the time of Jesus, David's line had regressed to the level of a peasant, no longer a princely line of one who would be raised in a palace. It belonged to one raised in a modest carpenter shop. Isaiah very distinctly declares that the shoot will spring "from the stem of Jesse."

Branch means a live sprout. This is the second time in our study we have identified a reference to the Branch. In Isaiah 53 we will see that He is "a root out of parched ground." The point is that Christ did have an humble beginning. He was born in the little town of Bethlehem, which was called the City of David, but it was also the city of Jesse.

Isaiah 11:2

The Spirit of the LORD will rest on Him, The spirit of wisdom and understanding, The spirit of counsel and strength, The spirit of knowledge and the fear of the LORD.

The seven-fold Spirit rested upon the Lord Jesus Christ, the abundance of power. We'll number these:

1: Of the Lord
2: Wisdom
3: Understanding
4: Counsel
5: Strength (or Might)
6: Knowledge
7: Fear of the Lord

The number seven in Scripture means "perfection, fullness, or completeness." No human could fulfill all of these qualities with perfection. Only One Person who has ever been on this earth has fulfilled this description perfectly and completely – the Lord Jesus Christ.

Isaiah 11:3-4

And He will delight in the fear of the LORD, And He will not judge by what His eyes see, Nor make a decision by what His ears hear; 4 But with righteousness He will judge the poor, And decide with fairness for the afflicted of the earth; And He will strike the earth with the rod of His mouth, And with the breath of His lips He will slay the wicked.

The wicked one, Satan, will have his time of influence on earth during the Great Tribulation. There will be no deliverance for the world during that time. Even Israel will cry out, but help will not come from the north, the south, the east, or the west. Help will come from above. At that time, after the Great Tribulation, the Messiah will come and begin His 1,000 year reign.

The reason for the Lord Jesus returning to earth is foretold all through the Old Testament Scriptures, as we have studied in these prophecies.

The world won't vote for Him to come, but God has voted for Him. This is God's universe – He owns everything in it – all that is here on the earth, and all that is in the universe. God will establish Messiah here on earth, to rule and to be our Judge. There will be no lengthy court case. There won't be any lawyers to intervene. There will be two judgments: one for believers, and one for unbelievers. It will be terrifying for those who do not know the LORD.

Every believer will stand before the LORD to answer for how they lived on this earth. At the beginning of the Tribulation, believers will be raptured (taken out of the world), brought into the presence of, and stand before the judgment seat of Christ. Then, 1,007 years later, the lost – the unbelievers – will face the great white throne-room judgment.

Isaiah 11:5
> Also righteousness will be the belt about His loins,
> And faithfulness the belt about His waist.

Characteristics of the LORD'S reign will be faithfulness and righteousness. The purpose of Christ's reign on earth will be to bring about uprightness and justice, as well as to restore the paradise that was lost by Adam.

Isaiah 11:6
> And the wolf will dwell with the lamb,
> And the leopard will lie down with the young goat,
> And the calf and the young lion [a]and the fatling
> together; And a little boy will lead them.

---

a. Isaiah 11:6 Some versions read *will feed together*

Isaiah 11:7
> Also the cow and the bear will graze,
> Their young will lie down together,
> And the lion will eat straw like the ox.

Knowing the nature of these animals, it is beyond our understanding how this can be. But God does things that we don't yet understand. Today the only way a lion and a young calf would lie down together would be if the calf was in the lion's belly!

Isaiah 11:9
> They will not hurt or destroy in all My holy mountain,
> For the earth will be full of the knowledge of the Lord
> As the waters cover the sea.

This indicates that Jesus' gentle nature will abound in all creatures. In Hebrew, "mountain" generally means "kingdom," thus the Lord's Kingdom will extend over the whole earth.

Isaiah 11:10
> Then in that day
> The nations will resort to the root of Jesse,
> Who will stand as a [a]signal for the peoples;
> And His resting place will be [b]glorious.

It is reiterated, "the nations will resort to the root of Jesse," referring to the line of David. The phrase "in that day" refers to the period of time which begins with the Tribulation and extends into the Millennial Kingdom. This verse confirms that the Gentiles (Christians) will be included in this Kingdom.

.

---

a. Isaiah 11:10 Or *standard*; b. Lit *glory*

Isaiah 25:6

The LORD of hosts will prepare a [a]lavish banquet for all peoples on this mountain; A banquet of [b]aged wine, [c]choice pieces with marrow, And [d]refined, aged wine.

Notice that "The LORD of hosts will prepare...for all peoples" wonderful things! We will have the "choice" – the very best – of everything. Certainly the earth will be very productive. There will be plenty of good food and drink. There is also a second meaning here in "marrow" – spiritual food. In our current human form, we need solid food and drink to sustain life. Spiritual food is very important to our soul's growth, and in that day we will hunger for spiritual things.

Isaiah 25:8

He will swallow up death for all time, And the Lord [e]GOD will wipe tears away from all faces, And He will remove the reproach of His people from all the earth; For the LORD has spoken.

This verse is referenced by Paul in his first letter to the church at Corinth.

1 Corinthians 15:54

But when this [f]perishable will have put on [g]the imperishable, and this mortal will have put on immortality, then will come about the saying that is written, "DEATH IS SWALLOWED UP in victory.

The LORD will reign in victory *Forever* — altogether triumphant.

---

a. Isaiah 25:6 Lit *feast of fat things*; i.e. abundance; b. Lit *wine on the lees*; c. Lit *fat pieces*; d. Lit *wine refined on the lees*
e. Isaiah 25:8 Heb *YHWH*, usually rendered LORD
f. 1 Corinthians 15:54 V 53, note 1; g. V 53, note 2

Isaiah 25:9

And it will be said in that day, "Behold, this is our God for whom we have waited that He might save us. This is the LORD for whom we have waited; Let us rejoice and be glad in His salvation."

As we come to this last stanza, attention is drawn to the person of God. The world will be deceived by Antichrist, but the real Christ – the true Messiah and final ruler of the earth – will come. Salvation will be vital to man in that day, and we who are believers will be glad and rejoice in the salvation we have through Jesus Christ.

Isaiah 26:1
Song of Trust in God's Protection

In that day this song will be sung in the land of Judah:

"We have a strong city;
He sets up walls and ramparts for [a]security.

Israel definitely doesn't sing this song today. The current conditions in the Middle East certainly are not a fulfillment of this particular prophecy.

Isaiah 28:16

Therefore thus says the Lord [b]GOD,

"Behold, I am laying in Zion a stone, a tested stone, A costly cornerstone for the foundation, [c]firmly placed. He who believes in it will not be [d]disturbed.

To what do we attribute the decline in morality? In lying? In cheating? In not accepting responsibility for what we do? It appears that the human condition will

---

a. Isaiah 26:1 Or *salvation*
b. Isaiah 28:16 Heb *YHWH*, usually rendered LORD; c. Lit *well-laid*; d. Lit *in a hurry*

continue to worsen as time progresses to the Great Tribulation. God has sent an Answer for us – One that takes care of all of our failings. Christ is the foundation, a tried stone, a precious cornerstone, a sure foundation. Those who believe in Him do not need to flee in sudden panic, or be dismayed. They can rest in Him, rather than in the flimsy base of their own accomplishments.

1 Peter 2:6-8

For *this* is contained in [a]Scripture:

> "BEHOLD, I LAY IN ZION A CHOICE *stone*, A PRECIOUS CORNER STONE, AND HE WHO BELIEVES IN [b]HIM WILL NOT BE [c]DISAPPOINTED."

7 This precious value, then, is for you who believe; but for those who disbelieve,

> "THE STONE WHICH THE BUILDERS REJECTED,
> THIS BECAME THE VERY CORNER *stone*,"

8 and,

> "A STONE OF STUMBLING AND A ROCK OF OFFENSE";

for they stumble because they are disobedient to the word, and to this *doom* they were also appointed.

Simon Peter draws a very clear picture for us. This is our Lord and Savior Jesus Christ. He is that Stone, our Rock, and our Salvation.

---

a. 1 Peter 2:6 Or *a scripture*; b. Or *it*; c. Or *put to shame*

CHAPTER 37: MESSIAH'S MIRACLES

The millennial rule of Christ will begin after the seven years of Tribulation. We never have to worry, even though we may be in the midst of the storm of judgment. If we belong to the kingdom of God, we can rejoice, because God will come to rescue us.

We who are in the Church – the body of believers – have an added hope and joy of never having to experience the Great Tribulation.

Isaiah 35:5-6
> Then the eyes of the blind will be opened
> And the ears of the deaf will be unstopped.
> 6 Then the lame will leap like a deer,
> And the tongue of the mute will shout for joy.
> For waters will break forth in the wilderness
> And streams in the [a]Arabah.

Sickness and disease are afflictions which are the result of man's sin, beginning with Adam and Eve and continuing to the present day. These judgments will be lifted in the Kingdom.

Let's look forward about 700 years, when Christ enters the picture.

Matthew 11:4-6
> Jesus answered and said to them,
> "Go and report to John what you hear and see:
> 5 the BLIND RECEIVE SIGHT and the lame walk,
> the lepers are cleansed and the deaf hear,
> the dead are raised up, and the POOR HAVE
> THE [b]GOSPEL PREACHED TO THEM. 6 And blessed
> is he [c]who does not [d]take offense at Me."

---

a. Isaiah 35:6 Or *desert*
b. Matthew 11:5 Or *good news*
c. Matthew 11:6 Lit *whoever*; d. Or *stumble over Me*

While John the Baptist was in prison he heard of the works of Christ. He sent two of his disciples to inquire of Him, was he "the Expected One, or do we look for someone else?"

Luke 7:19
> Summoning [a]two of his disciples, John sent them to the Lord, saying, "Are You the [b]Expected One, or do we look for someone else?"

Jesus is always the perfect example for us. These miracles are just a taste of what we will find in the Kingdom.

---

a. Luke 7:19 a. Lit *a certain two*; b. Lit *Coming One*

CHAPTER 38: MESSIAH'S HIGHWAY

This Scripture continues in the millennium.

Isaiah 35:8-10

A highway will be there, a roadway,
And it will be called the Highway of Holiness.
The unclean will not travel on it, But it *will* be for him
who walks *that* way, And fools will not wander *on it*. 9
No lion will be there, Nor will any vicious beast go up on
it; [a]These will not be found there. But the redeemed
will walk *there*, 10 And the ransomed of the LORD will
return And come with joyful shouting to Zion, With
everlasting joy upon their heads. They will [b]find
gladness and joy, And sorrow and sighing will flee away.

This is a wonderful picture of the Kingdom Age, or
millennium. It is a picture of perfection, and it includes
not only Israel, but all of the redeemed.

Zechariah 14:16-17

Then it will come about that any who are left of all the
nations that went against Jerusalem will go up from year
to year to worship the King, the LORD of hosts, and to
celebrate the Feast of Booths. 17 And it will be that
whichever of the families of the earth does not go up to
Jerusalem to worship the King, the LORD of hosts, there
will be no rain on them.

Not all of the people of the nations who are against
Israel in the end times will agree with their leaders.
Many will support Israel and will turn to God. A large
remnant – a huge multitude – will have specific
instructions to follow concerning the worship of the
Lord. This will be a time of testing.

---

a. Isaiah 35:9 Lit *It*
b. Isaiah 35:10 Lit *overtake*

CHAPTER 39: MESSIAH'S TENDERNESS

It is interesting that the Book of Isaiah is comprised of 66 chapters, which correspond to the 66 books of the Bible. Chapter 40 brings us to a major division of the book. A new, significantly different theme emerges with this chapter and continues through the rest of Isaiah.

The first 39 chapters of Isaiah are about judgment, history, and the government of God. They run parallel with the 39 books of the Old Testament. The next 27 chapters are about salvation and the grace of God – the theme of the 27 books of New Testament. Isaiah is, in a sense, a miniature Bible!

The chapters covered thus far have revealed the Sovereign upon the Throne. Now we will see the revelation of the Savior at Golgotha, the place of suffering. In Chapter 6 we saw the Crown; in Chapter 53 we will see the Cross.

Isaiah 40:5
[a]Then the glory of the LORD will be revealed,
And all flesh will see it together;
For the mouth of the LORD has spoken."

This verse reveals the Second Coming of the Lord.

Isaiah 40:9-10
Get yourself up on a high mountain, O Zion, bearer of good news, Lift up your voice mightily, O Jerusalem, bearer of good news; Lift it up, do not fear. Say to the cities of Judah, "Here is your God!" 10 Behold, the Lord [b]GOD will come with might, With His arm ruling for Him. Behold, His reward is with Him And His recompense before Him.

---

a. Isaiah 40:5 Or In order that the
b. Isaiah 40:10 Heb YHWH, usually rendered LORD

Isaiah 40:11

> Like a shepherd He will tend His flock,
> In His arm He will gather the lambs
> And carry *them* in His bosom;
> He will gently lead the nursing *ewes*.

Here we see Jesus, fulfilling His name, Emmanuel – God with us. He is the Good Shepherd in Psalm 23 – leading us beside the still waters, making us to lie down in green pastures, and causing our cup to overflow.

This is a wonderful picture of the coming Messiah – the Good Shepherd who died for His sheep.

CHAPTER 40: THE SERVANT OF JEHOVAH, JESUS

This is the first of four "Servant Songs" found in Isaiah.

Isaiah 42:1

"Behold, My Servant, whom I [a]uphold; My chosen one *in whom* My soul delights. I have put My Spirit upon Him; He will bring forth justice to the [b]nations.

Behold is a word which commands our undivided attention. In this case, God commands that we give our attention to His Son, in whom He delights. The Lord Jesus is the fulfillment of this prophecy. He brought justice to the Gentiles when He hung on the Cross.

Matthew 12:17-21

This was to fulfill what was spoken through Isaiah the prophet:

18 "BEHOLD, MY [c]SERVANT WHOM I [d]HAVE CHOSEN; MY BELOVED IN WHOM MY SOUL [e]IS WELL-PLEASED; I WILL PUT MY SPIRIT UPON HIM, AND HE SHALL PROCLAIM [f]JUSTICE TO THE [g]GENTILES. 19 "HE WILL NOT QUARREL, NOR CRY OUT; NOR WILL ANYONE HEAR HIS VOICE IN THE STREETS.
20 "A BATTERED REED HE WILL NOT BREAK OFF, AND A SMOLDERING WICK HE WILL NOT PUT OUT, UNTIL HE [h]LEADS [i]JUSTICE TO VICTORY. 21 "AND IN HIS NAME THE [j]GENTILES WILL HOPE."

---

a. Isaiah 42:1 Or *hold fast*; b. Or *Gentiles*
c. Matthew 12:18 Lit *Child*; d. Lit *chose*; e. Or *took pleasure*; f. Or *judgment*;
g. Or *nations*
h. Matthew 12:20 Or *puts forth*; i. Or *judgment*
j. Matthew 12:21 Or *nations*

Isaiah 42:2-3

"He will not cry out or raise *His voice*,
Nor make His voice heard in the street.
3 "A bruised reed He will not break
And a dimly burning wick He will not extinguish;
He will faithfully bring forth justice.

These verses very much depict the role of Jesus – characterizing His work and His life – when He was here on this earth as the Servant of Jehovah.

There is an old saying, "If you give someone enough rope, they will hang themselves." Meanwhile, they have a chance to straighten up and do right. The Lord did not force His way in to violently stop sin. He allows sin to bring its own judgment.

The person who continues in sin and does not change his ways will eventually break out in flames. The wages of sin is death – a penalty that will never change.

CHAPTER 41: A LIGHT TO THE GENTILES

Isaiah 42:6-7

"I am the LORD, I have called You in righteousness,
I will also hold You by the hand and watch over You,
And I will appoint You as a covenant to the people,
As a light to the nations, 7 To open blind eyes,
To bring out prisoners from the dungeon
And those who dwell in darkness from the prison.

He came as the Light of the World. Upon His return, He will bring out prisoners from the dungeon – those who live in darkness and sin.

Luke 2:29-32

"Now Lord, You are releasing Your bond-servant to depart in peace, According to Your word;
30 For my eyes have seen Your salvation,
31 Which You have prepared in the presence of all peoples, 32 A LIGHT [a]OF REVELATION TO THE GENTILES, And the glory of Your people Israel."

During Christ's 33 years on earth, He performed various miracles. Many are recorded in the Bible; however, there were more, too numerous to document.

John 20:30

Therefore many other [b]signs Jesus also performed in the presence of the disciples, which are not written in this book;

---

a. Luke 2:32 Or for
b. John 20:30 Or attesting miracles

CHAPTER 42: THE SUFFERING SERVANT

Isaiah 52:13-14 (NKJV)
The Sin-Bearing Servant

> Behold, My Servant shall [a]deal prudently;
> He shall be exalted and [b]extolled and be very high.
> 14 Just as many were astonished at you,
> So His visage[c] was marred more than any man,
> And His form more than the sons of men;

These two verses describe a very strange sequence of events. First, we are told that Christ "shall be exalted and extolled and be very high." Then in the next verse we witness the travail Christ endured – His Crucifixion – to fulfill His mission on earth.

The word "prudent" in some versions is translated "prosper" which means to be wise, successful, triumphant, or victorious. *Prudent* means to be careful or discreet, displaying wisdom, using common sense. A prudent person is careful to avoid being involved in embarrassing situations.

Many speak of being prudent in their conduct. We should ask whether or not our political leaders are prudent in all of their actions. If you ask one political party you will hear one answer. If you ask their opponents you will receive another answer. If you think the Republicans have been prudent ask the Democrats, or vice-versa. You will probably discover, if you read between the lines, that no one has been prudent.

Man today is not prudent, but when our Lord, Jesus Christ returns He will rectify this situation.

---

a. Isaiah 52:13 *prosper*
b. Lit. *be lifted up*
c. Isaiah 52:14 *appearance*

Verse 14 prepares us for the next chapter in Isaiah. It certainly depicts the Crucifixion of Christ. During that time of darkness when the activities of men stood still, Christ was at work on the Cross. It was during those hours of blackness that the Cross became an altar, and Christ – the Lamb of God – was paying for the sins of the world. That Perfect Sacrifice was dying for *our sins*.

After those hours of darkness, the crowd must have been startled when the light broke upon the Cross. The Christ on that Cross was so unspeakably disfigured that He did not appear to be human.

CHAPTER 43: THE MESSIAH SUFFERING

As we studied Psalm 22, which depicted the Crucifixion, we referred to Isaiah 53. These two chapters of the Old Testament present a vivid account of the Crucifixion of Christ – more vivid than is found elsewhere in the Bible. This may come as somewhat of a surprise to those of us who are accustomed to thinking that the four gospels alone describe the sorrowful, horrible death of the Son of God.

In examining the Gospel accounts, we find that only a few unrelated events connected with the Crucifixion are presented. The actual Crucifixion is not really emphasized, perhaps out of reverent restraint.

God, through the Holy Spirit, has thrown somewhat of a veil of silence over that event. In the Gospels, few of the lurid details are set forth for the curious to gaze upon. It is said the brutal crowd who murdered Jesus sat down to watch Him suffer and die. But God placed the cloak of darkness over His Son's agony.

He protected the sacredness of that event, not allowing it to be treated as commonplace. Also, it is quite possible that God did not want us to become too familiar with that which we have no need to know.

Once again, let us remember as we study the Crucifixion, it was prophesied hundreds of years *before* it actually happened. This cannot be overemphasized! The Crucifixion of Christ was, and is, the most important event in the history of man.

The first nine verses of Isaiah 53 tell of the suffering of the Savior. The rest of the chapter relates the satisfaction of the Savior. It is common sense that these two themes belong together: suffering and satisfaction.

I, and many of my friends and acquaintances have survived serious surgeries – heart bypass, tumor removals, etc. As each of us recovered and returned to our somewhat normal activities, we felt we had a new lease on life. We certainly found great satisfaction in recovering. I have had surgery on my lower back, and more recently, tumor removal and reconstructive surgery. I went through times of pain and suffering, but when my body was healed (with the Lord's help) I returned to my previous lifestyle. There was much gratification in getting through those ordeals.

There can be times of mental anguish as well. As we weather these challenges and later return to our normal lives we gain tremendous satisfaction. That contentment comes from knowing the Lord and relying on Him to see us through life's difficulties.

For instance, while in the Army I endured some pretty rigorous training. Every morning, there were two or three hours of PT (physical training) followed by a seven or eight mile run. Before reaching the end of that run I was suffering! But when I completed the run and began to recover and get my breath back, I experienced a high degree of satisfaction in the accomplishment.

Nearly everyone has gone through some sort of suffering in their life, followed by great satisfaction. This experience is commonly referred to as "the light at the end of the tunnel." Despite whatever suffering and satisfaction we may have experienced, we cannot even begin to relate what happened to us with what happened to our Lord and Savior.

Psalm 30:5
> For His anger is but for a moment,
> His favor is for a lifetime;
> Weeping may last for the night,
> But a shout of joy *comes* in the morning.

Isaiah 53:1
The Suffering Servant

> Who has believed our message?
> And to whom has the arm of the LORD been revealed?

Isaiah complained because his message was not believed. What was revealed to him was not received by men – often the situation when prophets spoke to men. No one wanted to listen.

Isaiah 6:9-10
> He said, "Go, and tell this people:
>
> 'Keep on listening, but do not perceive; Keep on looking, but do not understand.' 10 "Render the hearts of this people [a]insensitive, Their ears [b]dull, And their eyes [c]dim, Otherwise they might see with their eyes, Hear with their ears, Understand with their hearts, And return and be healed."

God told Isaiah that the people would not hear the message, and that his words would not be believed.

Isaiah 53:2
> For He grew up before Him like a tender [d]shoot, And like a root out of parched ground; He has no *stately* form or majesty That we should look upon Him, Nor appearance that we should [e]be attracted to Him.

Christ is described as a tender plant, growing out of dry, parched ground. This is life in a lifeless environment – a miracle.

Again, let us note that the line of David, at the time of the birth of Christ, was no longer a kingly line. The

---

a. Isaiah 6:10 Lit *fat*; b. Lit *heavy*; c. Lit *besmeared*
d. Isaiah 53:2 Lit *suckling*; e. Lit *desire*

family of David had been cut off from the kingship. They were more or less peasants. The nation of Israel, no longer free, had the boot of Rome upon its throat.

The Roman Empire produced no great civilizations. It was merely a good imitator of great civilizations. The moral foundation was practically non-existent, supplanted by the debauched, pleasure-loving lifestyles of the Empire's citizens – much like our country today. The religion of Israel had gone to seed. They performed empty rituals, and their hearts remained cold and indifferent. Thus comes the root out of parched ground.

Into this situation came Christ. He came from a noble family, but they were cut off from a nation that had become a servant to Rome. We might say the loveliest Flower of Humanity came from the driest spot of the world's history. (Perhaps this is why He is called the "Lily of the Valley.")

If you ever visit Arizona, you will find that it has very little greenery. Large portions of the state consist of dry desert land. Imagine walking along in a desert of Arizona, and suddenly spotting a big, juicy watermelon – growing out of that dry and dusty soil. You'd be amazed! It would be a miracle; it simply could not occur in such an environment without a miracle. He was a Tender Plant and He came forth from God.

In the last half of this verse, we are returned to the Crucifixion. The prophet immediately focuses our attention on Jesus' suffering and death upon the Cross. We see a very clear picture of what Christ endured on the Cross as we look at Psalm 22. He had been beaten, to the point that He was unrecognizable, before He was placed on the Cross. His bones had come out of joint as, in agony, He hung suspended by His arms.

He had been abandoned by men. His disciples had left Him. People turned their faces from Him – even the ones who loved Him – because they could not bear to see Him. He was despised by most of the crowd; they had no pity, watching and mocking Him as He suffered.

Isaiah 53:3

> He was despised and forsaken of men, A man of [a]sorrows and acquainted with [b]grief; And like one from whom men hide their face He was despised, and we did not esteem Him.

Several times throughout Scripture Christ is identified as a man of sorrows, acquainted with grief. This seems to infer that Christ was a very unhappy man while He was here on the earth; however, this is an incorrect assumption. To clarify – concerning the few isolated incidents that speak of His weeping – yes, He was unhappy about certain circumstances.

This verse describes Jesus as He was being led to the Crucifixion, after being scourged and forced to wear a crown of thorns. But His sorrow was not for Himself. It was for the people He asked His Father to forgive when He was on the Cross.

He wept over Israel. He wept over the death of Lazarus and the grief of his sisters and friends. The sorrow and grief He bore was not for Himself. He was supremely happy in His mission here on the earth.

Hebrews 12:2

> [c]fixing our eyes on Jesus, the [d]author and perfecter of faith, who for the joy set before Him endured the cross, despising the shame, and has sat down at the right hand of the throne of God.

The portraits of Christ which depict Him as long-faced and very sad are not a true representation. This

---

a. Isaiah 53:3 Or *pains*; b. Or *sickness*
c. Hebrews 12:2 Lit *looking to*; d. Or *leader*

verse dispels any doubt. The majority of His time here on earth was joyful. Picture the Cross as an altar on which He joyfully offered that perfect, satisfactory payment – the *only* acceptable payment – for the penalty of our sins.

This is not the end of the Gospel story! We certainly do not worship a dead Christ. We worship a living One. He not only died – He rose again from the grave. He rose in triumph. He was victorious over the world and over death, *FOREVER*. He ascended back to Heaven, and at this moment He is sitting at God's right hand.

Isaiah 53:4

> Surely our [a]griefs He Himself bore,
> And our [b]sorrows He carried;
> Yet we ourselves esteemed Him stricken,
> [c]Smitten of God, and afflicted.

He was "Smitten of God, and afflicted." Isaiah was intent on us not missing this point – so intent that he mentioned it three times.

> *"But the LORD has caused the iniquity of us all*
> *To [d]fall on Him." (v.6)*

> *"But the LORD was pleased To crush Him," (v.10)*

> *"[e]Putting Him to grief." (v.10)*

> [Italics added]

We're shocked to our very souls when we recognize that it was God the Father who treated the Perfect Man in such a terrible fashion. We don't understand it. We are led to question why God would treat His Son in this manner. God has revealed to us through the Old

---

a. Isaiah 53:4 Or *sickness*; b. Or *pains*; c. Or *Struck down by*
d. Isaiah 53:6 Lit *encounter Him*
e. Isaiah 53:10 Lit *He made Him sick*

Testament prophecies that He would be that Lamb, that Perfect Sacrifice, the only living being without blemish that would be acceptable to God for our iniquities.

Christ was on the Cross for six hours, hanging between heaven and earth from 9:00 in the morning until about 3:00 in the afternoon. In those first three hours, men did their worst. They heaped ridicule and insult upon Him, spit upon Him, without mercy nailed Him to that cruel Cross, and then sat down to watch Him die, mocking Him all the while.

At noon, after Jesus had hung there in agony for three hours, God drew a veil over His Son and darkness covered that scene, shutting out from human eyes the transaction between the Father and the Son. Jesus Christ, who was Perfect and knew no sin, was treated as sin. He was made (became) sin for us.

If you want to know what God thinks of sin, look at this event and imagine what it took for God to allow His own Son to be placed upon that Cross – to put Him through such unspeakable agony to pay for our sins.

Hebrews 2:3
> how will we escape if we neglect so great a salvation? [a]After it was at the first spoken through the Lord, it was confirmed to us by those who heard,

That Cross became a sacrificial altar where the Lamb of God took away the sin of the world. He was dying for others, including you and me. Listen to the prophet.

Isaiah 53:5
> But He was [b]pierced through for our transgressions, He was crushed for our iniquities; The chastening for our [c]well-being *fell* upon Him, And by His scourging we are healed.

---

a. Hebrews 2:3 Lit *Which was*
b. Isaiah 53:5 Or *wounded*; c. Or *peace*

The phrase, "by His scourging we are healed," brings a question to mind. Of what are we healed? Are we healed of physical diseases? Is that the primary meaning?

Peter makes it very clear that we are healed of our trespasses and sins.

1 Peter 2:24
> and He Himself [a]bore our sins in His body on the [b]cross, so that we might die to [c]sin and live to righteousness; for by His [d]wounds you were healed.

God made His Son an offering for our sin. Let's look again at Isaiah 53:6. It begins with "All". Not just some, but *all* of us have gone astray. The verse continues to say that all of our iniquity – *all* of our sin – was placed on Him.

Isaiah 53:6
> All of us like sheep have gone astray,
> Each of us has turned to his own way;
> But the LORD has caused the iniquity of us all
> To [e]fall on Him.

As we look at the Crucifixion of Christ, our hearts go out in sympathy. We feel sorry for Him. He expired upon that tree, and we're certainly not unmoved by such pain and suffering. However, Christ does not want our sympathy. He wants our hearts. He wants our love. He wants us to accept Him, and by accepting Him, He wants us to do His will.

---

a. 1 Peter 2:24 Or *carried...up to the cross*; b. Lit *wood*; c. Lit *sins*;
d. Lit wound; or welt
e. Isaiah 53:6 Lit *encounter Him*

Isaiah 53:11

As a result of the [a]anguish of His soul, He will see [b]*it and* be satisfied; By His knowledge the Righteous One, My Servant, will justify the many, As He will bear their iniquities.

The result of what He did is that down through the ages, multitudes have come to Him and found His saving grace – His pardon for their wrongdoing. He is a joyful Christ, and is even more joyful when we accept His gift of eternal life. He longs to give you this gift. He asks nothing in return. He wants to give you the most precious gift that can be given – more precious than silver and gold.

---

a. Isaiah 53:11 Or *toilsome labor*; b. Another reading is *light*

CHAPTER 44: THE COMING OF THE REDEEMER TO ISRAEL

Let's review a few points before we proceed to Chapter 60 of Isaiah. The charges against Israel were spelled out, as God reminded the people how they had been reduced to such a grim situation because of their sins. Their religion had become only a disguise for their sins. God refused to hear Israel call to Him because of their iniquities – not because He was hard of hearing.

We are generally disappointed when our prayers are not answered in the manner we would prefer, and so we think God has a hearing problem. The problem is not with God – the problem lies within us.

In this chapter, the sins of Israel are referenced 32 times. We will review a few.

Isaiah 59:1

Behold, the LORD's hand is not so short
That it cannot save; Nor is His ear so dull
That it cannot hear.

The LORD is still able to save His people. He has His full capabilities, as He has had from the beginning of time and will forever possess. The problem is deep within the human heart.

Isaiah 59:2

But your iniquities have made a separation between you and your God, And your sins have hidden His [a]face from you so that He does not hear.

When we dare compare ourselves to God, we are intimidated. Not just because God is so great, or because He lives forever and ever. Not even because He

---

a. Isaiah 59:2 So versions; M.T. *faces*

is omniscient (all-knowing). We compare how small we are, and how our lives are like a puff of smoke blown about by the wind.

We are separated from Him not because of how much He knows and how little we know, or because He is strong and we are weak. It is our sinful nature that has kept us from God.

Even so, there is a way for us to reach God. Christ is that *way*, but we must accept Him of our own free will; otherwise, we have no path to God. He gave us that perfect, unblemished sacrifice of His Son. We were bought at a great price.

John 14:6
Jesus *said to him, "I am the way, and the truth, and the life; no one comes to the Father but through Me.

Isaiah 59:9
A Confession of Wickedness

Therefore justice is far from us, And righteousness does not overtake us; We hope for light, but behold, darkness, For brightness, but we walk in gloom.

Isaiah includes himself in Israel's confession of sin. He looks forward to this Light which will come to Israel.

Isaiah 59:10
We grope along the wall like blind men, We grope like those who have no eyes; We stumble at midday as in the twilight, Among those who are vigorous *we are* like dead men.

This is a very good description of the person who does not have a personal relationship with the Lord. In darkness, one without Christ needs this great Light. As we review the list of Israel's problems, we cannot help but see some of our own. Until we have a personal relationship with Christ, we stumble in this same darkness.

Isaiah 59:20
"A Redeemer will come to Zion, And to those who turn from transgression in Jacob," declares the LORD.

Will all in the nation of Israel be saved? This question has been asked many times. The Redeemer is coming to Zion. At that time there will be a great confession of sin.

Zechariah 12:10
"I will pour out on the house of David and on the inhabitants of Jerusalem, [a]the Spirit of grace and of supplication, so that they will look on Me whom they have pierced; and they will mourn for Him, as one mourns for an only son, and they will weep bitterly over Him like the bitter weeping over a firstborn.

Many will receive the Holy Spirit – not only the inhabitants of Jerusalem – but those, wherever they may be, who belong to the house of David (Israel). This belief is further supported in the Book of Revelation.

Revelation 7:4
And I heard the number of those who were sealed, one hundred and forty-four thousand sealed from every tribe of the sons of Israel:

The LORD sealed 12,000 people from each of the 12 tribes of Israel. Some think this is the total number (144,000) who will be saved out of the Tribulation. But this group is unique for a much greater reason, as we learn in Revelation 14. The 144,000 are the witnesses who will convince the great multitude to accept Christ.

---

a. Zechariah 12:10 Or *a spirit*

Revelation 7:9
A Multitude from the Tribulation

> After these things I looked, and behold, a great
> multitude which no one could count, from every nation
> and *all* tribes and peoples and tongues, standing before
> the throne and before the Lamb, clothed in white robes,
> and palm branches were in their hands;

Note that God's Word says, "a great multitude which
no one could count" – of all nationalities – were
standing before the throne and the Lamb (Christ).

Revelation 7:13-14

> Then one of the elders answered, saying to me, "These
> who are clothed in the white robes, who are they, and
> where have they come from?" 14 I [a]said to him, "My
> lord, you know." And he said to me, "These are the ones
> who come out of the great tribulation, and they have
> washed their robes and made them white in the blood of
> the Lamb.

This presents a very clear description of the souls
who will be redeemed out of the Great Tribulation.

Revelation 14:1-2
The Lamb and the 144,000 on Mount Zion

> Then I looked, and behold, the Lamb *was* standing on
> Mount Zion, and with Him one hundred and forty-four
> thousand, having His name and the name of His Father
> written on their foreheads. 2 And I heard a voice from
> heaven, like the sound of many waters and like the
> sound of loud thunder, and the voice which I heard *was*
> like *the sound* of harpists playing on their harps.

---

a. Revelation 7:14 Lit *have said*

Revelation 14:3-5

And they *[a]sang a new song before the throne and
before the four living creatures and the elders; and no
one could learn the song except the one hundred and
forty-four thousand who had been purchased from the
earth. 4 These are the ones who have not been defiled
with women, for they [b]have kept themselves chaste.
These *are* the ones who follow the Lamb wherever He
goes. These have been purchased from among men as
first fruits to God and to the Lamb. 5 And no lie was
found in their mouth; they are blameless.

The 144,000 unique? Surely an understatement!

---

a. Revelation 14:3 Two early mss read *sing* something *like a new song*
b. Revelation 14:4 Lit *are chaste men*

CHAPTER 45: TO BE LIGHT OF THE WORLD

Christ will return to Jerusalem and establish His Millennial Kingdom at the end of the Tribulation – the end times. The remnant (144,000) will have finished their specific Tribulation mission of turning people to Christ.

If you are not caught up and taken out of this world in the Rapture, is that the end? Scripture supports that there will be a great turning to Christ during the Tribulation. Huge numbers of people will be saved (will come to know Jesus as their Lord and Savior) during that time, including many Jews. Even now, there are many Jewish Christians, often referred to as Messianic Jews. An even greater number will be converted during the Tribulation.

Chapter 59 of Isaiah closes with the Redeemer's future return to Zion. In Chapter 60, He has arrived. Prophecy emphasizes His return. Malachi said "the sun of righteousness will rise." (Malachi 4:2)

When Christ returns, it will be like the sun rising into the deep darkness of midnight.

Isaiah 60:1
"Arise, shine; for your light has come,
And the glory of the LORD has risen upon you.

John 8:12
Jesus Is the Light of the World

Then Jesus again spoke to them, saying, "I am the Light of the world; he who follows Me will not walk in the darkness, but will have the Light of life."

These Scriptures attest to the fact that Jesus is that *True Light* who came to earth (the first time) to seek and save the lost. God's Word says, "for your light has come, And the glory of the LORD has risen upon you." It doesn't say that your light *is* coming and that *it will* rise upon you – this has already happened. (Remember, this is prophecy to be fulfilled at the Second Coming of Christ.)

This great Glory and Light which will emanate from the Lord Jesus Christ will reflect over the entire earth, bringing it from darkness into light. This Light will particularly shine on the nation Israel, (still God's chosen people) including the remnant who will have survived the Tribulation.

It is important to remember that the Church (the worldwide body of believers) is not involved in this event. At this point, the Church has been raptured (taken out of the world) and is with Christ. Any attempt to involve the Church here does not coincide with the rest of prophecy, and is therefore misplaced. In fact, prophecy would have to be completely rewritten for this idea to fit, and we know that nothing can change that which God has written.

Isaiah 60:2
> "For behold, darkness will cover the earth
> And deep darkness the peoples;
> But the LORD will rise upon you
> And His glory will appear upon you.

A spiritual darkness is overtaking this present world, constantly growing and covering more of the earth with each passing day. Those of us who remember the last half of the 20th century and the beginning of the 21st century have witnessed this darkness insidiously encroach upon goodness. This is prophecy fulfilled.

The Word of God is more available today than it has ever been in the history of the world. Today, Bibles are being translated for people who do not even have a written language – the actual languages are being written in order to then provide them with Bibles.

We have the ability to reach the most remote corners of the world, through radio, television, printed materials, the Internet, missionaries – and more. Yet, in spite of the various methods now available to distribute and teach the Word of God, some people still do not believe. They prefer to live in darkness.

John 5:39-40
Witness of the Scripture

> [a]You search the Scriptures because you think that in them you have eternal life; it is these that testify about Me; 40 and you are unwilling to come to Me so that you may have life.

God intends for believers to take the Gospel – the Light – to everyone. This Light (Glory) is none other than Jesus Christ, our Kinsman-Redeemer.

Isaiah 60:3
> "Nations will come to your light,
> And kings to the brightness of your rising.

Nations and kings will be saved during the great revival of the Tribulation, including those from the nation Israel and from the rest of the world.

This earth is just one big graveyard. The billions of people who have died, and are either buried on land or at sea, or have had their ashes scattered, will be raised up at that time; some to be with the Lord, and some to be forever condemned.

---

a. John 5:39 Or (a command) *Search the Scriptures!*

Revelation 21:23-25

And the city has no need of the sun or of the moon to shine on it, for the glory of God has illumined it, and its lamp *is* the Lamb. 24 The nations will walk by its light, and the kings of the earth [a]will bring their glory into it. 25 In the daytime (for there will be no night there) its gates will never be closed;

---

a. Revelation 21:24 Lit *bring*

CHAPTER 46: JESUS AT NAZARETH

Jesus launched His public ministry in the synagogue in Nazareth, reading from Isaiah Chapter 61.

Isaiah 61:1-2
Exaltation of the Afflicted

> The Spirit of the Lord [a]GOD is upon me, Because the LORD has anointed me To bring good news to the [b]afflicted; He has sent me to bind up the brokenhearted, To proclaim liberty to captives And [c]freedom to prisoners; 2 To proclaim the favorable year of the LORD And the day of vengeance of our God; To comfort all who mourn,

Luke 4:16-21

> And He came to Nazareth, where He had been brought up; and as was His custom, He entered the synagogue on the Sabbath, and stood up to read. 17 And the [d]book of the prophet Isaiah was handed to Him. And He opened the [e]book and found the place where it was written,

> "THE SPIRIT OF THE LORD IS UPON ME,
> BECAUSE HE ANOINTED ME TO PREACH
> THE GOSPEL TO THE POOR. HE HAS SENT
> ME TO PROCLAIM RELEASE TO THE CAPTIVES,
> AND RECOVERY OF SIGHT TO THE BLIND,
> TO SET FREE THOSE WHO ARE OPPRESSED,

> 20 And He closed the [f]book, gave it back to the attendant and sat down; and the eyes of all in the synagogue were fixed on Him. 21 And He began to say to them, "Today this Scripture has been fulfilled in your [g]hearing."

---

a. Isaiah 61:1 Heb YHWH, usually rendered LORD; b. Or humble;
c. Lit opening to those who are bound
d. Luke 4:17 Or scroll; e. Or scroll
f. Luke 4:20 Or scroll
g. Luke 4:21 Lit ears

This passage in Isaiah, repeated in Luke, is extremely important. Jesus read verse one, and only part of verse two. It is remarkable that He did not finish the second verse. When Jesus read from Isaiah that day, a portion of prophecy was fulfilled in the sight and hearing of all who were present.

There is a 2000+ year lapse between the time He fulfilled the first part of this prophecy and the time the last part of verse two will be fulfilled. The remainder of verse two will be fulfilled at Christ's Second Coming.

CHAPTER 47: A NEW NAME

All Christian believers look forward with great anticipation to the return of Christ. This world will not remain as we now know it – everything will be new and different.

Isaiah 62:2

The nations will see your righteousness,
And all kings your glory;
And you will be called by a new name
Which the mouth of the LORD will designate.

When Christ returns, we will have a new Jerusalem and a new earth. Our bodies will be new, and we will even have a new name.

Revelation 2:17

He who has an ear, let him hear what the Spirit says to the churches. To him who overcomes, to him I will give some of the hidden manna, and I will give him a white stone, and a new name written on the stone which no one knows but he who receives it.'

CHAPTER 48: THE WINEPRESS OF JUDGMENT

In Chapter 53 of Isaiah, we studied how our Savior died on the Cross. He placed Himself at the mercy of the world. He was cruelly beaten; He was treated with utter contempt. His unimaginable suffering upon that shameful Cross *for us* is beyond our comprehension.

Now as we see Him in this 63rd chapter, He sits in judgment. This Christ (as Judge) will be entirely different from the Christ (as Savior) in Chapter 53. In His First Coming, Jesus endured unspeakable atrocities so that we might have a way to God – *if* we accept Him. In Chapter 63, it is too late. For those who still remain on this earth and have not accepted Him, time will have run out.

Isaiah 63:2

Why is Your apparel red, And Your garments like the one who treads in the wine press?

Winemaking in Isaiah's day was much different from today. There were no crushers and hydraulic presses. Grapes were placed in a huge vat and trampled underfoot to squeeze out the juice. During this trampling of the grapes, as grape juice and pulp sprang from the hulls, garments became stained. Notice the indication of "one" having trodden the winepress.

Isaiah 63:3

"I have trodden the wine trough alone,
And from the peoples there was no man with Me.
I also trod them in My anger
And trampled them in My wrath;
And their [a]lifeblood is sprinkled on My garments, And I [b]stained all My raiment.

---

a. Isaiah 63:3 Lit *juice*; b. Lit *defiled*

This time, it is the blood of Christ's enemies being shed – not His blood. It is the fulfillment of the second half of the second verse in Chapter 61. Let's review.

Isaiah 61:2

To proclaim the favorable year of the LORD
And the day of vengeance of our God;
To comfort all who mourn,

[Italics added.]

This is the fulfillment of prophecy, as the next verse supports.

Isaiah 63:4

"For the day of vengeance was in My heart, And My year of redemption has come.

Perhaps you have heard the old saying, "Vengeance is mine, saith the Lord," which is actually taken from Scripture (see Deuteronomy 32:35; Romans 12:19; Hebrews 10:30). This is the time when vengeance will be heaped upon all who have not repented of their wrongdoing, and have not asked Jesus Christ to be their Lord and Savior.

CHAPTER 49: THE RIGHTEOUSNESS OF GOD'S JUDGMENT

Why did God reject the nation Israel and reach out to the Gentile people? Throughout this study we have seen Israel reject Christ, and ultimately crucify Him.

John 1:1-5
The Deity of Jesus Christ

> In the beginning was the Word, and the Word was with God, and the Word was God. 2 [a]He was in the beginning with God. 3 All things came into being through Him, and apart from Him nothing came into being that has come into being. 4 In Him was life, and the life was the Light of men. 5 The Light shines in the darkness, and the darkness did not [b]comprehend it.

John 1:11

> He came to His [c]own, and those who were His own did not receive Him.

In the beginning the Word (Jesus) comes out of eternity. The beginning depicts the creation of the heavens and the earth, but He was already there. Our mathematical limitations will not allow us to determine the beginning when He, or the world, was made. No dates are given. Dates mean nothing to God – He is eternal, with no beginning and no end.

God, the Word (Jesus) and the Spirit of God are the Father, the Son, and the Holy Spirit.

Jesus has stated over and over again that He is the Light of the world. This is supported by our studies. He is the Light of the world – the only True Light.

---

a. John 1:2 Lit *This one;*
b. John 1:5 Or *overpower*
c. John 1:11 Or *own things, possessions, domain*

He came into the world as a baby and was placed in a manger (an animal feeding trough) in Bethlehem. Remember the shepherds (seemingly unimportant people) were first notified. God knew He would not be recognized by His own people.

Thus we have the darkness. It was in the world then, and it remains in the world today. From the beginning, darkness has the result of mankind's sin – the willful disregard of God's Word. The Jewish people, His *chosen people*, did not receive Him.

Isaiah 65:1
A Rebellious People

> "I permitted Myself to be sought by those who did not ask *for Me*; I permitted Myself to be found by those who did not seek Me. I said, 'Here am I, here am I,' To a nation which did not call on My name.

The Gospel – the Good News – has been brought to many who did not ask for it, who did not seek God. Through the ages, God has reached out to a people (the Gentiles) who did not know His name. We are included.

Consider the Parable of the Great Supper.

Luke 14:16-19
But He said to him, "A man was giving a big dinner, and he invited many; 17 and at the dinner hour he sent his slave to say to those who had been invited, 'Come; for everything is ready now.' 18 But they all alike began to make excuses. The first one said to him, 'I have bought a [a]piece of land and I need to go out and look at it; [b]please consider me excused.' 19 Another one said, 'I have bought five yoke of oxen, and I am going to try them out; [c]please consider me excused.'

---

a. Luke 14:18 Or *field*; b. Lit *I request you*
c. Luke 14:19 Lit *I request you*

> 20 Another one said, 'I have married a wife, and for that reason I cannot come.'

Invitations (the Messianic prophecies) to a supper (salvation) had been sent, far in advance. As the day for the supper arrived, a personal invitation was also extended.

God's invitation is for salvation, and you come to this supper by the grace of God. The invitation asks you to accept a gift – to receive Christ as your Lord and Savior. The only thing that will exclude anyone from heaven is their refusal to accept this gift.

Romans 1:16

> For I am not ashamed of the gospel, for it is the power of God for salvation to everyone who believes, to the Jew first and also to the Greek.

People make all kinds of excuses. In this parable, the first person to be invited refused because he had to go see about his newly purchased field. He could have been honest and admitted that he didn't want to come to supper, but instead he made this excuse. And it wasn't even a good excuse! Supper took place during the hours of darkness. It would have been very difficult to view a piece of land in the dark!

The next person who received an invitation begged off because he had bought a team of oxen and wanted to try them out. This excuse did not make sense either. To test oxen, they would first need to be hooked to a plow. It was dark. There were no electric lights, no floodlights. How could he see to hook up the team, and to plow?

A newlywed was the third person invited. He also declined. What man could go to a great supper without taking his new bride?

As we examine these flimsy excuses, perhaps some of our own come to mind. God has given us an engraved invitation, written in Christ's precious blood. It should be written on our hearts.

Our Lord has given us an invitation. What will you do with this invitation?

Luke 14:21-24

And the slave came *back* and reported this to his master. Then the head of the household became angry and said to his slave, 'Go out at once into the streets and lanes of the city and bring in here the poor and crippled and blind and lame.' 22 And the slave said, 'Master, what you commanded has been done, and still there is room.' 23 And the master said to the slave, 'Go out into the highways and along the hedges, and compel *them* to come in, so that my house may be filled. 24 For I tell you, none of those men who were invited shall taste of my dinner.'"

If you reject God's invitation, He will reject you. You will be excluded *only* because you did not accept the greatest gift of Christ's death on the Cross for you; *only* because you refused His invitation.

God rejected the nation Israel and reached out to the Gentile people. Only those who reject Him – who do not accept His gift, Christ the Lord – will be excluded.

CHAPTER 50: THE BRANCH

Jeremiah, often called the "Weeping Prophet," prophesied for approximately 39 years, from 626 to 587 BC. He wrote two of the five books of the major prophets – Jeremiah and Lamentations. Most of his rather unenviable task was to proclaim God's judgment on an unrepentant nation (Israel). He even remained celibate as a sign that judgment would come during his lifetime. It surely did! Yet, God gives some hope – that light at the end of the tunnel – as we see in Chapter 23.

Jeremiah 23:4-6

I will also raise up shepherds over them and they will [a]tend them; and they will not be afraid any longer, nor be terrified, nor will any be missing," declares the LORD.

5 "Behold, *the* days are coming," declares the LORD, "When I will raise up for David a righteous [b]Branch; And He will reign as king and [c]act wisely And do justice and righteousness in the land. 6 "In His days Judah will be saved, And Israel will dwell securely; And this is His name by which He will be called, 'The LORD our righteousness.'

Solomon's line was rejected because of all the evil kings it produced. Can anyone thwart God's purpose? Many people think they can, but that will never happen! God knows exactly what He will do. From the New Testament, we know that another branch in the line of Nathan – another son of David – produced the King. A peasant girl named Mary, a virgin who lived in Nazareth, bore Jesus. The Messiah. The King.

---

a. Jeremiah 23:4 Or *shepherd*
b. Jeremiah 23:5 Lit *Sprout*; c. Or *succeed*

Matthew 4:17

> From that time Jesus began to [a]preach and say,
> "Repent, for the kingdom of heaven is at hand."

There can't be a kingdom without a king. Jesus was declaring, "your King is here!" The people rejected Him, but He had the last word.

"The LORD our righteousness" – for indeed, the only righteousness we have is the righteousness of Jesus Christ – is one of His names. Gloriousness will characterize Christ's Kingdom.

To confirm this Scripture, let's look again at Isaiah.

Isaiah 4:2

> In that day the Branch of the LORD will be beautiful and glorious, and the fruit of the earth *will be* the pride and the adornment of the survivors of Israel.

---

a. Matthew 4:17 Or *proclaim*

CHAPTER 51: THE PRINCE OF THE HOUSE OF DAVID

Ezekiel, another of the major prophets, grew up in Jerusalem. In his early years, he served as a priest in the temple. He and King Jehoiachin were included in the second group of captives taken to Babylon. A contemporary of Daniel, (who had been held captive in Babylon for nine years) Ezekiel also became a prophet of God while in Babylon.

Ezekiel's ministry, like that of many other prophets, began with the condemnation and judgment of the nation Israel. By Chapter 33, and continuing to Chapter 39, his message became that of the restoration of Israel. These verses pertain specifically to the coming King – the Second Coming of Christ.

Ezekiel 37:24-25
The Davidic Kingdom

> "My servant David will be king over them, and they will all have one shepherd; and they will walk in My ordinances and keep My statutes and observe them. 25 They will live on the land that I gave to Jacob My servant, in which your fathers lived; and they will live on it, they, and their sons and their sons' sons, forever; and David My servant will be their prince forever.

In these verses, the shepherd David is none other than the Lord Jesus Christ. He was born into the line of David. Chapter 1 of Matthew and Chapters 1 and 2 of Luke very carefully record this fact.

Let's again refer to Isaiah. (It is no wonder he was called the Messianic Prophet!)

Isaiah 40:11

> Like a shepherd He will tend His flock, In His arm
> He will gather the lambs And carry *them* in His bosom;
> He will gently lead the nursing *ewes*.

Our Lord Jesus took the title of "Shepherd" in His First Coming.

John 10:11

> "I am the good shepherd; the good shepherd lays
> down His life for the sheep.

John 10:15

> even as the Father knows Me and I know the Father;
> and I lay down My life for the sheep.

In this Second Coming, He will be our Sovereign King and the Great Shepherd.

CHAPTER 52: THE LIFE-GIVING STREAM

As we have progressed through this study, we have concentrated mainly on the Old Testament. Yet the Old Testament and New Testament are continually linked, through prophecies and fulfillment of prophecies.

John 4:13-14

Jesus answered and said to her, "Everyone who drinks of this water will thirst again; 14 but whoever drinks of the water that I will give him shall never thirst; but the water that I will give him will become in him a well of water springing up to eternal life."

Jesus, speaking to the woman at the well, explained the difference between the water she drew from the well and the *Living Water*. This *Living Water* is the life-giving stream that flows from the Holy Spirit.

As Jesus spoke to the crowds, and to the Pharisees, He spoke of the promise of the indwelling Holy Spirit for those who believe in Him.

John 7:37-38

Now on the last day, the great *day* of the feast, Jesus stood and cried out, saying, "[a]If anyone is thirsty, [b]let him come to Me and drink. 38 He who believes in Me, as the Scripture said, 'From [c]his innermost being will flow rivers of living water.'"

In Ezekiel, we find described an actual river of living water, which heals all life that it touches. It also depicts the Holy Spirit which will flow to all people in the last days.

---

a. John 7:37 Vv 37-38 may also be read: *If anyone is thirsty,...let him come..., he who believes in me as...*; b. Or *let him keep coming to Me and let him keep drinking*
c. John 7:38 Lit *out of his belly*

Ezekiel 47:1-2
Water from the Temple

> Then he brought me back to the door of the house; and behold, water was flowing from under the threshold of the house toward the east, for the house faced east. And the water was flowing down from under, from the right side of the house, from south of the altar. 2 He brought me out by way of the north gate and led me around [a]on the outside to the outer gate by way of *the gate* that faces east. And behold, water was trickling from the south side.

The temple on Mount Zion is the location where the river of life (or life-giving stream) will originate, from the throne of God and the Lamb. We see this throne as an altar – the altar where all of our blessings originate.

Don't think of this as the altar in a church or other place of worship. Our altar is the Lord Jesus Christ and His Cross, His Millennial Throne. It will be the altar where all the people who are left on earth will worship Him. The healing water depicts the Holy Spirit.

Ezekiel 47:3-5

> When the man went out toward the east with a line in his hand, he measured a thousand cubits, and he led me through the water, water *reaching* the ankles. 4 Again he measured a thousand and led me through the water, water *reaching* the knees. Again he measured a thousand and led me through *the water*, water *reaching* the loins. 5 Again he measured a thousand; *and it was* a river that I could not ford, for the water had risen, *enough* water to swim in, a river that could not be forded.

Water rose up to the ankles, then to the knees, and finally to the waist. The farther one moved into the

---

a. Ezekiel 47:2 Lit *by way of*

stream, the deeper it became. There are no limits to the blessings of the Holy Spirit which will flow from His throne. All will be healed by this life-giving stream.

The ankle suggests the walk of the believer. As we are immersed up to our knees, we are immersed in prayer. Throughout Scripture we are instructed to "gird up our loins" for service, up to our waist. The service of a believer rests upon the redemption we have in Christ. The water, (the Holy Spirit) is limitless.

Ezekiel 47:6-7
He said to me, "Son of man, have you seen *this*?" Then he brought me [a]back to the bank of the river. 7 Now when I had returned, behold, on the bank of the river there *were* very many trees on the one side and on the other.

The great number of trees on each bank of the river is also depicted in Revelation.

Revelation 22:2
in the middle of its street. On either side of the river was the tree of life, bearing twelve [b]*kinds* of fruit, yielding its fruit every month; and the leaves of the tree were for the healing of the nations.

Zechariah 14:16-17
Then it will come about that any who are left of all the nations that went against Jerusalem will go up from year to year to worship the King, the Lord of hosts, and to celebrate the Feast of Booths. 17 And it will be that whichever of the families of the earth does not go up to Jerusalem to worship the King, the Lord of hosts, there will be no rain on them.

---

a. Ezekiel 47:6 Lit *and caused me to return*
b. Revelation 22:2 Or crops of *fruit*

As we look back through the Old Testament, we see that God often sent drought to punish nations. Without rain, no food was grown; livestock suffered. In the Millennial rule of Christ, the people who remain on earth after the Tribulation will have come to believe in Christ. (This does not include those who were raptured.)

Because the temple and throne will be located in Jerusalem, everyone will go there to worship and to be healed from any physical problems.

As we continue to delve into Scripture it becomes obvious that the stream flowing from the altar is an actual, physical stream – as well as a spiritual one.

Ezekiel 47:8-9

> Then he said to me, "These waters go out toward the eastern region and go down into the Arabah; then they go toward the sea, being made to flow into the sea, and the waters *of the sea* become [a]fresh. 9 It will come about that every living creature which swarms in every place where the [b]river goes, will live. And there will be very many fish, for these waters go there and *the others* [c]become fresh; so everything will live where the river goes.

This water, as well as being a depiction of the Holy Spirit, is a healing water. As the water flows into the streams and into the sea, the sea and all the creatures in the sea will be healed. Today our oceans and streams are polluted with waste created by humans. In addition to industrial and agricultural pollution, plastic waste is becoming a serious concern. The bodies of water on earth are certainly not in the pristine condition as they were when God created them. They need healing!

---

a. Ezekiel 47:8 Lit *healed*
b. Ezekiel 47:9 Lit *two rivers*; c. Lit *are healed*

Ezekiel 47:12

> By the river on its bank, on one side and on the other, will grow all *kinds of* trees for food. Their leaves will not wither and their fruit will not fail. They will bear every month because their water flows from the sanctuary, and their fruit will be for food and their leaves for healing."

The river of life which flows from the throne of God will be lined on both sides with all kinds of trees. Their leaves will not die, and their plentiful fruit will not fall to the ground. They will bear fruit continuously, because the water they receive (those unlimited blessings) flows from God's throne. Their fruit will serve for food, and their leaves for the healing of all nations (not just Israel).

CHAPTER 53: THE FOUR KINGDOMS OF THE WORLD AND THE FINAL KINGDOM

Daniel, sometimes referred to as "The Apocalypse of the Old Testament," was written over a period of some 65 years, between 605-540 BC. Daniel prophesied under the reigns of Nebuchadnezzar and Belshazzar (Babylonians), Darius the Mede, and Cyrus the Persian.

When Nebuchadnezzar first besieged Jerusalem, he deported Daniel and some of the other young men to Babylon to be trained for service in his government.

Daniel and his friends, devout Jewish teenagers, were ordered to compromise their faith by eating Babylonian food – much of which was considered unclean by the Jewish faith. Daniel requested that he and his friends be fed vegetables instead of the rich Babylonian food. The chief official, afraid the young men would grow weak and thin, reluctantly agreed to a trial period of ten days. At the end of the trial period, with God's provision, the young men were in much better condition than those who dined on the royal diet.

Daniel is a great book of history, written in *advance*. His narrative in Chapter 2 concerns Nebuchadnezzar's dream and the multi-metallic image.

Daniel 2:1
The King's Forgotten Dream

> Now in the second year of the reign of Nebuchadnezzar, Nebuchadnezzar [a]had dreams; and his spirit was troubled and his sleep [b]left him.

Babylon was the first world kingdom. Nebuchadnezzar, king of the entire known world, understood that his

---

a. Daniel 2:1 Lit *dreamed dreams*; b. Lit *was gone upon him* dreams were significant. He became so concerned about his kingdom that he could not sleep.

Daniel 2:2

Then the king [a]gave orders to call in the [b]magicians, the conjurers, the sorcerers and the [c]Chaldeans to tell the king his dreams. So they came in and stood before the king.

The king summoned his cabinet – men of high intellect, the astrologers and sorcerers who were somewhat equivalent to scientists and astronomers of our day – and gave them a unique command.

Daniel 2:3-5

The king said to them, "I [d]had a dream and my spirit [e]is anxious to [f]understand the dream."

4 Then the Chaldeans spoke to the king in [g]Aramaic: "O king, live forever! Tell the dream to your servants, and we will declare the interpretation." 5 The king replied to the Chaldeans, "[h]The command from me is firm: if you do not make known to me the dream and its interpretation, you will be [i]torn limb from limb and your houses will be made a rubbish heap.

Nebuchadnezzar was very anxious to know the meaning of his dream. The Chaldeans (some of his cabinet) immediately wanted him to reveal to them the details of the dream, which would then enable them as "experts" to interpret it. But Nebuchadnezzar refused to divulge the specifics.

---

a. Daniel 2:2 Lit *said to call*; b. Or *soothsayer priests*; c. Or *master astrologers*, and so throughout the ch
d. Daniel 2:3 Lit *dreamed*; e. Lit *was troubled*; f. Lit *know*
g. Daniel 2:4 The text is in Aramaic from here through 7:28
h. Daniel 2:5 Another reading is *The word has gone from me*; i. Lit *made into limbs*

In the sixth verse Nebuchadnezzar offered great gifts and honor to anyone who could correctly interpret the dream. Again in verse seven the wise men asked to know the dream so that they might give their interpretation.

Daniel 2:8

The king replied, "I know for certain that you are [a]bargaining for time, inasmuch as you have seen that [b]the command from me is firm,

Nebuchadnezzar realized the wise men were stalling.

Daniel 2:9

that if you do not make the dream known to me, there is only one [c]decree for you. For you have agreed together to speak lying and corrupt [d]words before me until the [e]situation is changed; therefore tell me the dream, that I may know that you can declare to me its interpretation."

The king knew that a true "seer" would be able to reveal the actual dream and its meaning. He lacked confidence in these wise men. Perhaps they had failed him previously, just as the prophets of Baal failed Ahab.

Daniel 2:10

The Chaldeans answered [f]the king and said, "There is not a man on earth who could declare the matter [g]for the king, inasmuch as no great king or ruler has *ever* asked anything like this of any [h]magician, conjurer or Chaldean.

Finally the wise men displayed some wisdom. No man on earth could have known the dream. The king's command was unreasonable.

a. Daniel 2:8 Lit *buying*; b. V 5, note 1
c. Daniel 2:9 Or *law*; d. Lit *word*; e. Lit *time*
f. Daniel 2:10 Lit *before the*; g. Lit *of*; h. Or *soothsayer priest*

Daniel 2:11

Moreover, the thing which the king demands is [a]difficult, and there is no one else who could declare it [b]to the king except gods, whose dwelling place is not with *mortal* flesh."

The wise men admitted that no human could meet the king's demands, and they had received no help from their gods. This provided an opening for Daniel.

Daniel 2:12

Because of this the king became indignant and very furious and gave orders to destroy all the wise men of Babylon.

Nebuchadnezzar was well known for his violent temper – a symptom of the psychosis he suffered.

Daniel 2:13

So the [c]decree went forth that the wise men should be slain; and they looked for Daniel and his friends to [d]kill *them*.

Nebuchadnezzar's decree included Daniel and his friends, since they were being trained in Babylonian ways by the same wise men that the king ordered destroyed.

Daniel 2:14-15

Then Daniel replied with discretion and discernment to Arioch, the captain of the king's [e]bodyguard, who had gone forth to slay the wise men of Babylon; 15 he said to Arioch, the king's commander, "For what reason is the [f]decree from the king so [g]urgent?" Then Arioch informed Daniel about the matter.

---

a. Daniel 2:11 Or *rare*; b. Lit *before*
c. Daniel 2:13 Or *law*; d. Lit *be killed*
e. Daniel 2:14 Or *executioners*
f. Daniel 2:15 Or *law*; g. Or *harsh*

Arioch, captain of the guard and a reasonable man, explained the situation. Daniel was amazed by the king's decree.

Daniel 2:16

So Daniel went in and requested of the king that he would [a]give him time, in order that he might declare the interpretation to the king.

Nebuchadnezzar, even in his unreasonable state, granted Daniel an audience. Daniel convinced the king to allow him time to interpret the dream. Nebuchadnezzar evidently sensed that Daniel was not stalling, and he agreed to an extension.

Daniel 2:17-18

Then Daniel went to his house and informed his friends, Hananiah, Mishael and Azariah, about the matter, 18 so that they might request compassion from the God of heaven concerning this mystery, so that Daniel and his friends would not be destroyed with the rest of the wise men of Babylon.

Daniel met with his friends, Shadrach, Meshach and Abednego (their Babylonian names) to fervently pray for God's intervention in this matter.

Daniel 2:19
The Secret Is Revealed to Daniel

Then the mystery was revealed to Daniel in a night vision. Then Daniel blessed the God of heaven;

God revealed all of the details of Nebuchadnezzar's dream to Daniel, and with the details also the interpretation.

---

a. Daniel 2:16 Or *appoint a time for him*

Daniel 2:20-23

Daniel said,

"Let the name of God be blessed forever and ever, For wisdom and power belong to Him. 21 "It is He who changes the times and the epochs; He removes kings and [a]establishes kings; He gives wisdom to wise men And knowledge to [b]men of understanding. 22 "It is He who reveals the profound and hidden things; He knows what is in the darkness, And the light dwells with Him. 23 "To You, O God of my fathers, I give thanks and praise, For You have given me wisdom and power; Even now You have made known to me what we requested of You, For You have made known to us the king's matter."

Daniel was a man of purpose, a man of prayer, and a man of prophecy. This prayer of thanksgiving is one of his several recorded prayers.

Daniel 2:24

Therefore, Daniel went in to Arioch, whom the king had appointed to destroy the wise men of Babylon; he went and spoke to him as follows: "Do not destroy the wise men of Babylon! Take me [c]into the king's presence, and I will declare the interpretation to the king."

In an effort to prevent the bloody slaughter that was about to take place, Daniel told Arioch he was ready to interpret the king's dream.

Daniel 2:25

Then Arioch hurriedly brought Daniel [d]into the king's presence and spoke to him as follows: "I have found a man among the [e]exiles from Judah who can make the interpretation known to the king!"

---

a. Daniel 2:21 Or *sets up*; b. Lit *knowers*
c. Daniel 2:24 Lit *in before the king*
d. Daniel 2:25 Lit *in before the king*; e. Lit *sons of the exile of*

Arioch quickly brought Daniel to Nebuchadnezzar, with the promise the interpretation would be revealed.

Daniel 2:26

> The king said to Daniel, whose name was Belteshazzar, "Are you able to make known to me the dream which I have seen and its interpretation?"

Daniel, a young trainee, said he had the answers. The king, with perhaps a bit of sarcasm, said, 'You mean to tell me that all the other wise men had no answer but you think you can answer me?' He was very skeptical of Daniel's abilities.

Daniel 2:27-28

> Daniel answered before the king and said, "As for the mystery about which the king has inquired, neither wise men, conjurers, [a]magicians *nor* diviners are able to declare *it* to the king. 28 However, there is a God in heaven who reveals mysteries, and He has made known to King Nebuchadnezzar what will take place in the [b]latter days. This was your dream and the visions [c]in your mind *while* on your bed.

Note that even as Daniel provided the wise men of Babylon an excuse, he clearly pointed out the distinctive difference between their wisdom and the wisdom of God. Daniel had the unique opportunity of introducing to the mind of this pagan king the living and true God. The dream Daniel interpreted for the king was a preview of a large segment of world history.

---

a. Daniel 2:27 Or *soothsayer priests*
b. Daniel 2:28 Lit *end of the days*; c. Lit *of your head*

Daniel 2:29

As for you, O king, *while* on your bed your thoughts [a]turned to what would take place [b]in the future; and He who reveals mysteries has made known to you what will take place.

Previously a minor king with a minor kingdom, Nebuchadnezzar was now the ruler of the entire known world. The dream left him with great concern for the future of his now mighty kingdom.

The Gentiles ruled the world at this point in time because of the failure of Israel. God had taken the scepter of the world from the hands of the line of David and placed it in the hands of the Gentiles. It will remain with the Gentiles until the Second Coming of Christ, when as rightful owner, He will claim the scepter and rule on this earth as King of kings and Lord of lords.

Daniel 2:30

But as for me, this mystery has not been revealed to me for any wisdom [c]residing in me more than *in* any *other* living man, but for the purpose of making the interpretation known to the king, and that you may [d]understand the thoughts of your [e]mind.

Nebuchadnezzar was right to be concerned; the dream depicted the eventual downfall of his great kingdom. It prophetically outlined the succession of events to come – major events that would become world history.

Daniel disclaimed any credit for himself, and hoped to protect the lives of the wise men, as he emphasized that only God in heaven could have revealed the dream. God spoke to Nebuchadnezzar (a Gentile) in a language he would understand.

---

a. Daniel 2:29 Lit *came up*; b. Lit *after this*
c. Daniel 2:30 Lit *which is*; d. Lit *know*; e. Lit *heart*

Daniel 2:31

> "You, O king, were looking and behold, there was a
> single great statue; that statue, which was large and
> [a]of extraordinary splendor, was standing in front of
> you, and its appearance was awesome.

Babylon was known at that time as the center of
pagan religion, where the people worshiped a multitude
of idols. Because Nebuchadnezzar did fall down to
worship before the images (idols) in the city of Babylon,
God used an image in the dream. This "language" made
it easier for the king to understand as Daniel explained.

Daniel began to describe the image in Nebuchadnezzar's dream – a mighty image that inspired fear and
respect. Perhaps it was difficult for the king to believe
that someone could know what he had dreamed, but
the fact that Daniel could recount the dream lent
confidence that his interpretation would be accurate.

Daniel 2:32-33

> The head of that statue *was made* of fine gold, its breast
> and its arms of silver, its belly and its thighs of bronze,
> 33 its legs of iron, its feet partly of iron and partly of
> clay.

The idol was composed of a strange assortment of
metals and clay, with its head of gold, chest and arms of
silver, belly and thighs of bronze, legs of iron, and feet
of iron and clay. It was not an alloy of metals – each
section was distinct.

Nebuchadnezzar must have been amazed as Daniel
continued to relay the exact details of the dream.

---

a. Daniel 2:31 Lit *its splendor was surpassing*

Daniel 2:34-35

You [a]continued looking until a stone was cut out without hands, and it struck the statue on its feet of iron and clay and crushed them. 35 Then the iron, the clay, the bronze, the silver and the gold were crushed [b]all at the same time and became like chaff from the summer threshing floors; and the wind carried them away so that not a trace of them was found. But the stone that struck the statue became a great mountain and filled the whole earth.

It is important to note that Nebuchadnezzar beheld the image with a sense of awe and wonder. Gold, silver and bronze were known for their strength and malleability. Iron, while somewhat brittle, was also strong. Clay was a common building material. All were known for their durability.

Suddenly a stone appeared, separate from the statue, that was not of human origin. It smote the feet of iron and clay with such force that the entire image was destroyed. All of the metals and clay were completely pulverized – crushed into a fine dust. Then a wind blew the dust away. No trace of the image remained.

The stone, as if living, grew to fill the entire world, replacing the great image.

Daniel 2:36-37

"This *was* the dream; now we will tell its interpretation before the king. 37 You, O king, are the king of kings, to whom the God of heaven has given the [c]kingdom, the power, the strength and the glory;

---

a. Daniel 2:34 Lit *were*
b. Daniel 2:35 Lit *like one*
c. Daniel 2:37 Or *sovereignty*

Daniel 2:38
> and wherever the sons of men dwell, *or* the beasts of
> the field, or the birds of the sky, He has given *them* into
> your hand and has caused you to rule over them all. You
> are the head of gold.

The head of gold represented King Nebuchadnezzar, the first "world" ruler. God had given him authority over all that He had given Adam authority over in the beginning – the animals of the field and the fowl of heaven. Jeremiah further substantiates this.

Jeremiah 27:5-7
> "I have made the earth, the men and the beasts which
> are on the face of the earth by My great power and by
> My outstretched arm, and I will give it to the one who is
> [a]pleasing in My sight. 6 Now I have given all these lands
> into the hand of Nebuchadnezzar king of Babylon, My
> servant, and I have given him also the wild animals of
> the field to serve him. 7 All the nations shall serve him
> and his son and his grandson until the time of his own
> land comes; then many nations and great kings will
> [b]make him their servant.

Jeremiah's message here was not just for Israel. Written around 600 BC – a few years before Israel went into captivity under Babylonian rule – it was a prophecy concerning all the kingdoms of the world.

Daniel 2:39
> After you there will arise another kingdom inferior to
> you, then another third kingdom of bronze, which will
> rule over all the earth.

The next section represented the Medo-Persian Empire (Darius and Cyrus), which Daniel noted as being inferior to the head of gold. Nevertheless, they

---

a. Jeremiah 27:5 Or *upright*
b. Jeremiah 27:7 Or *enslave him*

would rule the known world at that time. God revealed, through Daniel, the future of the Babylonian kingdom.

Daniel 5:28

'PERĒS'—your kingdom has been divided and given over to the Medes and [a]Persians."

Daniel lived in Babylon during both kingdoms. King Darius signed a decree that eventually caused Daniel to come face-to-face with some hungry lions.

Daniel 6:8

Now, O king, establish the injunction and sign the document so that it may not be changed, according to the law of the Medes and Persians, which [b]may not be revoked."

We all know the story of Daniel and the lion's den. This just further supports the fact that he was there during the time of the Medo-Persian rule.

The third kingdom is easy to decipher; it is the kingdom of Alexander the Great. Upon his death, his kingdom – the Greco-Macedonian Empire of Alexander the Great – would be split into four separate kingdoms.

Daniel 2:40-41
Rome

Then there will be a fourth kingdom as strong as iron; inasmuch as iron crushes and shatters all things, so, like iron that breaks in pieces, it will crush and break all these in pieces. 41 In that you saw the feet and toes, partly of potter's clay and partly of iron, it will be a divided kingdom; but it will have in it the toughness of iron, inasmuch as you saw the iron mixed with [c]common clay.

---

a. Daniel 5:28 Aram: *Pāras*
b. Daniel 6:8 Lit *does not pass away*
c. Daniel 2:41 Lit *clay of mud*

Daniel 2:42-43

> As the toes of the feet were partly of iron and partly of pottery, so some of the kingdom will be strong and part of it will be brittle. 43 And in that you saw the iron mixed with [a]common clay, they will combine with one another [b]in the seed of men; but they will not adhere to one another, even as iron does not combine with pottery.

Much detail is provided concerning this fourth kingdom, which is the kingdom that still exists today. Although much weaker than it was in those past glory days, there is indication that at some point this kingdom will again become strong. Many Bible scholars believe this will be the revival of the Roman Empire. Thinking of the Roman Empire perhaps brings to mind Italy; however, when Rome was the world ruler their kingdom extended into Britain and all of Europe – all of the known world.

God revealed to Nebuchadnezzar the future – what would become world history. Envision again the multi-metallic image of Nebuchadnezzar's dream. The head of gold that represents Babylon; the breast and arms of silver that represents Medo-Persia; the brass that represents the Greco-Macedonian Empire of Alexander the Great; the legs of iron that represents Rome in its earlier days; and the feet of clay attached to the iron legs which depicts the last form of the Roman Empire.

What is the reason for the particular order in the quality of metals in this image? I believe it indicates, as time advances, a definite degrading in the quality of the metals. First, gold, followed by silver, brass, iron, and iron and clay. We can see the specific deterioration of these metals; therefore, deterioration in the kingdoms. Noting the condition of these countries today, we see that Rome is the only one that remains virtually intact.

---

a. Daniel 2:43 Lit *clay of mud*; b. Or *with*

Perhaps reminding us of the well known children's tale of "Humpty-Dumpty" who fell off the wall, the once strong Roman Empire basically fell apart. A lot of men have tried, unsuccessfully, to put it together again. It was one of the first missions of the Roman Catholic Church. Charlemagne sought to put it back together. Napoleon tried to do so. Hitler and Mussolini both attempted. So far, the man has not appeared who will accomplish this feat. God is not quite ready for him to appear, but it could happen at any time.

In the latter days, growth and expansion will occur. The seat of government may be in Rome, or it may be elsewhere, but I believe that the old kingdom will be re-established. Antichrist, the man of sin, (he has many different identities in Scripture) is the one who will re-establish the Roman Empire. He will be a dictator who will rule over the world just as Nebuchadnezzar did all those centuries ago. In Revelation 13, we see an ideal form of government, with the wrong man at the top. It will be a dreadful period of time, filled with unimaginable atrocities. This was true of Nebuchadnezzar's reign, and will certainly be true of the Antichrist's dominion.

In these next verses, we see that the final Kingdom will be set up with that stone cut out not by human hands. When Jesus returns, He will be an autocratic ruler, the Perfect Dictator.

Daniel 2:44

> In the days of those kings the God of heaven will set up a kingdom which will never be destroyed, and *that* kingdom will not be [a]left for another people; it will crush and put an end to all these kingdoms, but it will itself endure forever.

---

a. Daniel 2:44 Or *passed on to*

Daniel 2:45

Inasmuch as you saw that a stone was cut out of the mountain without hands and that it crushed the iron, the bronze, the clay, the silver and the gold, the great God has made known to the king what will take place [a]in the future; so the dream is true and its interpretation is trustworthy."

Cut out of the mountain without human hands, the stone represents none other than our Lord and Savior, Jesus Christ. He is God's anointed one. Jesus Himself made it clear – He is that stone.

Psalm 2:9

'You shall [b]break them with a [c]rod of iron,
You shall shatter them like [d]earthenware.'"

Matthew 21:44

And he who falls on this stone will be broken to pieces; but on whomever it falls, it will scatter him like dust."

He is that Rock of salvation, and He is also the Rock of judgment. As we think about this stone, let's focus on coming to that stone and falling over it; not coming to the stone and letting it fall upon us in judgment.

---

a. Daniel 2:45 Lit *after this*
b.Psalm 2:9 Another reading is *rule*; c. Or *scepter* or *staff*; d. Lit *potter's ware*

CHAPTER 54: THE MINOR PROPHETS

Hosea is the first of the twelve minor prophets. Though they are designated as "minor" because of the length of their prophetic writings, they each deliver a powerful message.

Hosea and Amos (a contemporary prophet of Hosea) served in the northern kingdom of Israel before and up to the time of their captivity by Assyria. Hosea had the unenviable position of being ordered by God to choose a prostitute as a wife. This symbolized the sinful nation of Israel and their harlotry towards God.

Hosea and his wife, Gomer, had three children. The first child was a son named Jezreel. His name meant "God will scatter" and "God will avenge." The second child was a daughter, Lo-Ruhamah. Her name meant she "never knew a father's pity." It was not that she was an orphan; rather, the identity of her father was not known. God's message to the people of the northern kingdom was, "You will not know my pity, for I am not your Father." The third child, a son, was named Lo-Ammi, which means "not my people." If we convert this to the singular it means "not my child." Quite a message in Hosea's day! We might relate it to today's liberal theologians who claim that everyone is a child of God.

John 8:44
> You are of *your* father the devil, and you want to do the desires of your father. He was a murderer from the beginning, and does not stand in the truth because there is no truth in him. Whenever he speaks [a]a lie, he speaks from his own *nature*, for he is a liar and the father of [b]lies.

---

a. John 8:44 Lit *the lie*; b. Lit *it*

Unless we have accepted Jesus as our personal Savior, we are illegitimate children. On the other hand...

John 1:12
> But as many as received Him, to them He gave the right to become children of God, *even* to those who believe in His name,

The story of Hosea's troubled home continues. Gomer left home and returned to the "oldest profession in the world," once again becoming a common prostitute. The LORD instructed Hosea to not only bring his wife back, but to love her. Since she had been sold into slavery, he had to purchase her freedom for the price of six ounces of silver and five quarts of barley.

We see in this story that even though God was merciful to the nation Israel and claimed them as His chosen people, they had sinned and committed adultery against Him. Even at this, He blessed them. He brought them out of Egypt when they were slaves, and settled them in a new land. Still, down through the years, they continued to sin again and again. God allowed other nations, as the names of Hosea's children depict, to scatter Israel, though He avenged Israel when those nations were unmerciful.

Throughout His judgments, God displayed mercy. Scattering and disclaiming Israel as His people, calling them illegitimate, we see in the Books of Prophecy that Israel will be forgiven and restored.

CHAPTER 55: RESTORATION OF ISRAEL

Hosea 1:10

[a]Yet the number of the sons of Israel
Will be like the sand of the sea,
Which cannot be measured or numbered;
And in the place
Where it is said to them,
"You are not My people,"
It will be said to them,
"You are the sons of the living God."

Throughout Israel's history, the Hebrew people have been persecuted – decimated time and time again. To consider just one instance, remember Hitler's genocide of the Jewish population of Europe, when an estimated six million Jews were systematically murdered. Yet, here is God's marvelous promise to Abraham. God always delivers what He promises. We know, in no uncertain terms, that God is not through with Israel – His chosen people.

Genesis 22:17-18

indeed I will greatly bless you, and I will greatly multiply your [b]seed as the stars of the heavens and as the sand which is on the seashore; and your [c]seed shall possess the gate of [d]their enemies. 18 In your [e]seed all the nations of the earth shall [f]be blessed, because you have obeyed My voice."

---

a. Hosea 1:10 Ch 2:1 in Heb
b. Genesis 22:17 Or *descendants*; c. Or *descendants*; d. Lit *his*
e. Genesis 22:18 Or *descendants*; f. Or *bless themselves*

CHAPTER 56: OUT OF EGYPT

Hosea 11:1
> When Israel *was* a youth I loved him,
> And out of Egypt I called My son.

Looking 700 years beyond the time this was written, we see that the Magi – or "Wise Men" as they are now popularly called – came from the east to seek the Child born in Bethlehem. When they went to King Herod in search of the Child, he instructed them to return after they found Him, so he, too, could go and worship Him. Of course, we all know Herod had an ulterior motive. He did not like competition.

Matthew 2:13
> Now when they had gone, behold, an angel of the Lord *appeared to Joseph in a dream and said, "Get up! Take the Child and His mother and flee to Egypt, and remain there until I tell you; for Herod is going to search for the Child to destroy Him."

God warned Joseph to take Jesus to safety in Egypt, which was certainly unusual, because God usually cautioned people to stay out of Egypt. This escape protected Jesus from Herod's murderous decree (see verses 16-18) when he ordered that all male children two years old and under be put to death.

Matthew 2:14-15
> So [a]Joseph got up and took the Child and His mother while it was still night, and left for Egypt. 15 He [b]remained there until the death of Herod. *This was* to fulfill what had been spoken by the Lord through the prophet: "OUT OF EGYPT I CALLED MY SON."

---

a. Matthew 2:14 Lit *he*
b. Matthew 2:15 Lit *was*

The LORD God sent His Son into the safety of Egypt, there to remain until the threat of Herod was gone. When Herod died, God called His Son out of the relative safety of Egypt and into the eventual danger He would ultimately face on the Cross to pay for our disobedience.

Remember God brought Israel out of Egypt, out of danger, and into the safety that He provided. Here God called His Son out of Egypt and into the dangerous situation He would face not just for the salvation of Israel and the Hebrew people, but for the salvation of all people. That includes you and me.

CHAPTER 57: THE GOSPEL ERA

The Book of Joel, likely written between 835-800 BC, was named after its author who has been called the "Prophet of Pentecost." Joel's prophecy concerned Jerusalem, confirmed as he referred again and again to the House of the LORD – the temple in Jerusalem.

Chapter 2, verses 28-32 are subtitled "The Promise of the Holy Spirit." The future time called the day of the LORD will begin with the dark years of the Tribulation. After this, Christ will return and establish His Kingdom on the earth.

Joel 2:28-32
The Promise of the Spirit

> 28 "[a]It will come about after this
> That I will pour out My Spirit on all [b]mankind;
> And your sons and daughters will prophesy,
> Your old men will dream dreams,
> Your young men will see visions.
> 29 "Even on the male and female servants
> I will pour out My Spirit in those days.

The Day of the LORD

> 30 "I will display wonders in the sky and on the earth,
> Blood, fire and columns of smoke. 31 "The sun will be turned into darkness And the moon into blood
> Before the great and awesome day of the LORD comes.
> 32 "And it will come about that whoever calls on the name of the LORD Will be delivered; For on Mount Zion and in Jerusalem There will be those who escape,
> As the LORD has said, Even among the survivors whom the LORD calls.

---

a. Joel 2:28 Ch 3:1 in Heb; b. Lit *flesh*

In studying this prophecy it is important to note the time frame indicated in the Scripture itself. Note that in the first verse it says, "It will come about after this."

It is pointed out that this period of time will begin with the seven year Tribulation or "darkness." After this, the children of Israel – many of them – will turn and seek the LORD their God and will worship Jesus on bended knee. Joel speaks of a very definite period of time, which leads us to conclude that he is speaking of a time that prophecy will be fulfilled, during the day of the LORD, after the darkness of the Great Tribulation.

Remember that the Church has already been taken up in the Rapture, before the Tribulation. The people involved in this prophecy are those who are left on the earth. Dwell on Verse 32 for a moment. "And it will come about That whoever calls on the name of the LORD Will be delivered." This is a very late date to be calling on the name of the LORD. Hopefully, most people will have already done so. This verse does not specify just the Jewish people (to whom this was primarily written); rather, it pertains to all those who survive the Tribulation.

Ezekiel 39:28-29

> Then they will know that I am the LORD their God because I made them go into exile among the nations, and then gathered them *again* to their own land; and I will leave none of them there any longer. 29 I will not hide My face from them any longer, for I will have poured out My Spirit on the house of Israel," declares the Lord GOD.

At the end of the Great Tribulation, the LORD'S chosen people who have been scattered all around the earth will return to their homeland. Even those who have been held in captivity, or in countries where leaving is difficult, will return to Israel. The LORD will no longer hide His face from them. He will pour out His Spirit on the house of Israel. This is the very same time frame, after the Tribulation, described in Joel 2:28-32.

Ezekiel 36:24-28

For I will take you from the nations, gather you from all the lands and bring you into your own land. 25 Then I will sprinkle clean water on you, and you will be clean; I will cleanse you from all your filthiness and from all your idols. 26 Moreover, I will give you a new heart and put a new spirit within you; and I will remove the heart of stone from your flesh and give you a heart of flesh. 27 I will put My Spirit within you and cause you to walk in My statutes, and you will be careful to observe My ordinances. 28 You will live in the land that I gave to your forefathers; so you will be My people, and I will be your God.

At the end of the Tribulation, the LORD will return to judge the nations.

Joel 3:11-14

[a]Hasten and come, all you surrounding nations,
And gather yourselves there. Bring down, O LORD,
Your mighty ones. 12 Let the nations be aroused
And come up to the valley of [b]Jehoshaphat,
For there I will sit to judge
All the surrounding nations.
13 Put in the sickle, for the harvest is ripe.
Come, tread, for the wine press is full;
The vats overflow, for their wickedness is great.
14 Multitudes, multitudes in the valley of [c]decision! For the day of the LORD is near in the valley of [d]decision.

---

a. Joel 3:11 Or *Lend aid*
b. Joel 3:12 I.e. YHWH judges
c. Joel 3:14 I.e. God's verdict; d. I.e. God's verdict

Again, remember the time frame. These are the people who have survived the Great Tribulation. The day of the LORD has arrived, when He will judge the remainder of the nations. Look for a moment at a portion of Jesus' Olivet Discourse.

Matthew 25:31-41
The Judgment

31 "But when the Son of Man comes in His glory, and all the angels with Him, then He will sit on His glorious throne. 32 All the nations will be gathered before Him; and He will separate them from one another, as the shepherd separates the sheep from the goats; 33 and He will put the sheep on His right, and the goats on the left.

34 "Then the King will say to those on His right, 'Come, you who are blessed of My Father, inherit the kingdom prepared for you from the foundation of the world. 35 For I was hungry, and you gave Me *something* to eat; I was thirsty, and you gave Me *something* to drink; I was a stranger, and you invited Me in; 36 naked, and you clothed Me; I was sick, and you visited Me; I was in prison, and you came to Me.' 37 Then the righteous will answer Him, 'Lord, when did we see You hungry, and feed You, or thirsty, and give You *something* to drink? 38 And when did we see You a stranger, and invite You in, or naked, and clothe You? 39 When did we see You sick, or in prison, and come to You?' 40 The King will answer and say to them, 'Truly I say to you, to the extent that you did it to one of these brothers of Mine, *even* the least *of them*, you did it to Me.' 41 "Then He will also say to those on His left, 'Depart from Me, accursed ones, into the eternal fire which has been prepared for the devil and his angels;

These verses in Matthew describe in detail what will happen to those who have not used their resources wisely to assist His people. Also noted is the treatment of the 144,000 – those who will take His Word to the world during the Tribulation. They will be persecuted as no other group has been persecuted in the history of the world. Anyone who assists these people by giving them a drink of water, food, shelter or meeting their other needs will be blessed. However, in so doing they will place themselves in grave danger.

Even though not in the group Raptured, a great multitude of people will turn to Christ during this time. When Jesus speaks of the harvest, He is referencing the end of the age or the day of the LORD. These passages in Joel tell us that the day of the LORD begins after the Rapture of the Church, with a Great Tribulation, and continues through the Second Coming of Christ. As He establishes His Kingdom, He will judge who will be allowed to enter the Kingdom. This is another very clear and concise picture of what will happen as the day of the LORD arrives.

CHAPTER 58: DAVID'S FALLEN THRONE TO RISE

A shepherd and fruit picker from the Judean village of Tekoa (due south of Bethlehem), Amos was very reluctant to answer God's call. He lacked an education or a priestly background, yet God gave him a mission and a message for his northern neighbor, Israel. Found in the ninth chapter of Amos, this message was one of impending gloom and captivity for the nation.

This prophecy was directed to the people because of their extensive neglect of God's Word – their idolatry, pagan worship, greed, corrupted leadership, oppression of the poor, and more. The message was very unpopular and fell on deaf ears.

Not since the days of Solomon had Israel enjoyed such prosperity, as Jeroboam the Second reigned over Israel, and Asa reigned over Judah.

Amos began by pronouncing a judgment on all the surrounding nations, then upon his own nation of Judah and, finally, the harshest judgment on Israel. His visions from God revealed the emphatic message that judgment was near.

In this short synopsis of Chapter 9, these important verses conclude the message of judgment upon Israel, ending as Amos predicts the future glorious prospect of the restored kingdom of Israel.

Amos 9:8-9

"Behold, the eyes of the Lord God are on the sinful kingdom, And I will destroy it from the face of the earth; Nevertheless, I will not totally destroy the house of Jacob," Declares the Lord. 9"For behold, I am commanding, And I will shake the house of Israel among all nations As *grain* is shaken in a sieve, But not a [a]kernel will fall to the ground.

---

a. Amos 9:9 Or *pebble*

Amos 9:10-12

"All the sinners of My people will die by the sword,
Those who say, 'The calamity will not overtake or
confront us.'

The Restoration of Israel

11 "In that day I will raise up the fallen [a]booth of David,
And wall up its breaches; I will also raise up its ruins
And rebuild it as in the days of old;
12 That they may possess the remnant of Edom
And all the [b]nations who are called by My name,"
Declares the LORD who does this.

In the eighth verse, God said He would destroy the sinful kingdom, wiping it off of the face of the earth. The people would be scattered and Israel would no longer exist as a separate kingdom. Following, in the ninth verse, God said He would shake (sift, as in a sieve) the house of Israel among all the nations.

The Jewish people are scattered throughout the world. The northern kingdom is sometimes referred to as the "ten lost tribes." They may be lost to us, but they are not lost to God. Verse nine continues, "not a kernel will fall to the ground." God will not lose a single one of His chosen people.

Verse 10 warns, "All the sinners of My people will die by the sword...." God will judge the people who don't turn to Him. The same situation exists in our churches today. Not all church members are saved; just because they are church members does not mean they are members of the family of God. Some churches are in trouble. Unbiblical practices are taking place with the approval of church leadership.

---

a. Amos 9:11 Or *shelter* or *tabernacle*
b. Amos 9:12 Or *Gentiles*

This brings us to the next two verses, where we see the worldwide regathering and restoration of the Kingdom of the LORD. When God returns the people of Israel to their land they will be one nation under the sovereignty of the One who will be sitting on the throne of David – Jesus Christ our Savior.

Amos saw the light at the end of the tunnel. He saw beyond the dire days of judgment and scattering of his people. He saw beyond the Great Tribulation, still in the future. We hear the phrase again, "In that day," which refers to the last days of Israel. God said He would raise up the booth (or tabernacle) of David which was fallen. To follow through on this, James quoted Amos.

Acts 15:13-18
James's Judgment

> 13 After they had stopped speaking, [a]James answered, saying, "Brethren, listen to me. 14 Simeon has related how God first concerned Himself about taking from among the Gentiles a people for His name. 15 With this the words of the Prophets agree, just as it is written,
>
>> 16 'AFTER THESE THINGS I will return,
>> AND I WILL REBUILD THE [b]TABERNACLE OF DAVID WHICH HAS FALLEN, AND I WILL REBUILD ITS RUINS, AND I WILL RESTORE IT, 17 SO THAT THE REST OF [c]MANKIND MAY SEEK THE LORD, AND ALL THE GENTILES [d]WHO ARE CALLED BY MY NAME,' 18 SAYS THE LORD, WHO [e]MAKES THESE THINGS KNOWN FROM LONG AGO.

James said, "KNOWN FROM LONG AGO" are all His works – from the beginning of time. Today God is calling out a people for His name among the Gentiles.

---

a. Acts 15:13 Or *Jacob*
b. Acts 15:16 Or *tent*
c. Acts 15:17 Gr *anthropoi*; d. Lit *upon whom My name is called*
e. Acts 15:18 Or *does these things* which *were known*

Amos 9:12 mentions the remnant of Edom. Esau was Jacob's brother. There will be a remnant of Esau's descendants who will turn to the LORD in those last days – all the Gentiles who are called by God's name. No matter the nationality, they will be saved. There will be a great multitude of people saved out of the Tribulation.

After this He will raise up the Tabernacle of David, which is the Kingdom of Christ. This is known as the "Kingdom Age" or "Millennium" – which is the blessed future for those who have trusted Jesus as their Savior.

CHAPTER 59: THE RELUCTANT PROPHET

Background on Jonah reveals that he was the only Old Testament prophet from Galilee. Born in Israel, he grew up in a city called Gath Hepher, about three miles from Nazareth. God's commission for Jonah was that he go to the Gentile nation of Assyria, specifically to the capital city, Nineveh, to preach repentance. This was a hard pill to swallow for Jonah, since the Assyrians were very brutal and oppressive, and long-standing enemies of Israel. Not only afraid to go there, he had an extreme dislike for the Assyrians. Jonah did not want to preach to them, because he truly did not want them to repent. He thought they should be punished. So rather than go to Nineveh as God instructed, he went in the opposite direction by boarding a ship bound for Tarshish.

During the voyage, a violent storm arose, so intense, the crew feared the ship would break up and they would all drown. In an effort to determine the reason for the storm, the crew cast lots and determined that Jonah was the cause. After confronting him and asking what he had done, Jonah confessed that he had disobeyed the LORD. He told the crew to throw him overboard, but they were reluctant to do so and attempted to row back to land. Realizing they could not reach land, and after begging God to not hold it against them, they tossed Jonah into the raging sea which instantly calmed.

Jonah was swallowed and remained in the belly of a large fish for three days and three nights.

Jonah 1:17
[a]And the LORD appointed a great fish to swallow Jonah, and Jonah was in the stomach of the fish three days and three nights.

---

a. Jonah 1:17 Ch 2:1 in Heb

Indeed a miracle, the LORD prepared a great fish specifically for the purpose of swallowing Jonah. Please note that Scripture does not say whether Jonah was alive during his time inside that fish, so there is a great deal of conjecture about whether he was alive or dead while in the belly of this creature. Whether or not he was alive, the Lord commanded the fish to vomit Jonah onto dry land. At this point, Jonah was obviously alive.

Jonah 2:10

Then the Lord commanded the fish, and it vomited Jonah up onto the dry land.

Some say, "It just goes to show you can't keep a good man down." Others have said that even a fish couldn't digest Jonah, the "Backsliding Prophet." Regardless, Jonah underwent a major attitude adjustment on the way down, and in the belly of the giant fish he made a new pact with the LORD. Jonah prayed, God heard, and He delivered Jonah from the great fish.

Recorded by Luke and Matthew, in His interview with the scribes and Pharisees, Jesus spoke of Jonah's three days and three nights in the belly of the great fish.

Matthew 12:38-40
The Desire for Signs

38 Then some of the scribes and Pharisees said to Him, "Teacher, we want to see a [a]sign from You." 39 But He answered and said to them, "An evil and adulterous generation craves for a [b]sign; and yet no [c]sign will be given to it but the [d]sign of Jonah the prophet; 40 for just as JONAH WAS THREE DAYS AND THREE NIGHTS IN THE BELLY OF THE SEA MONSTER, so will the Son of Man be three days and three nights in the heart of the earth.

a. Matthew 12:38 I.e. attesting miracle
b. Matthew 12:39 I.e. attesting miracle; c. I.e. attesting miracle; d. I.e. attesting miracle

Here the scribes and Pharisees attempted to trick Jesus. They appeared to fall in step with Jesus by asking Him for a sign. Of course, they had no intention of believing because of a sign. This was just another endeavor to trap Him.

There is a major distinction between how Jonah finally complied with the will of God – very reluctantly – compared to Jesus, who willingly suffered without complaint.

Luke 11:29-32
The Sign of Jonah

> 29 As the crowds were increasing, He began to say, "This generation is a wicked generation; it seeks for a [a]sign, and *yet* no [b]sign will be given to it but the [c]sign of Jonah. 30 For just as Jonah became a [d]sign to the Ninevites, so will the Son of Man be to this generation. 31 The Queen of the South will rise up with the men of this generation at the judgment and condemn them, because she came from the ends of the earth to hear the wisdom of Solomon; and behold, something greater than Solomon is here. 32 The men of Nineveh will stand up with this generation at the judgment and condemn it, because they repented at the preaching of Jonah; and behold, something greater than Jonah is here.

The sign Jesus referred to in this passage was His resurrection from the grave after three days and three nights. He mentioned two incidents in the Old Testament. First, the account of the prophet Jonah, who was apparently raised from the dead after being in the belly of the fish. God brought him out of darkness and death into light and life. Jonah's experience was indicative of the coming death and resurrection of our Lord and Savior Jesus Christ.

---

a. Luke 11:29 Or *attesting miracle*; b. Or *attesting miracle*; c. Or *attesting miracle*
d. Luke 11:30 Or *attesting miracle*

When Jonah finally followed God's instruction, His message to the Ninevites was positively received. They listened to his preaching, took it to heart, fasted, and in sackcloth and ashes, repented. The acts of Israel as a nation put her in a much worse position. She did not receive her messenger, even though she was much more exposed to the Word of God and the prophecies than was Nineveh.

CHAPTER 60: UNCOMMON PROPHESY FOR THE COMMON PEOPLE

Micah was a prophet of the common people. Rugged, direct and convincing, he was from the prominent Judean city of Moresheth, about 25 miles southwest of Jerusalem. Micah's ministry spanned the reigns of Jotham, Ahaz, and Hezekiah. These were years of great oppression and corruption – turbulent times. The people were being exploited. Israel and Judah were both deep in sin, despite their wealth. Micah's message of imminent judgment upon them was very unpopular and much resented.

The Book of Micah was written to both Israel and Judah. Its message was directed against the people in Samaria, the northern capital, and Jerusalem, the capital of the southern kingdom. Corrupt rulers, false prophets, ungodly priests, and cheating merchants were significant reasons for God's coming judgment against the nations.

Even so, as in all the Books of Prophecy, God demonstrated His merciful grace – a promise of the future restoration of the Jewish nation. In the midst of their destruction, Micah prophesied the birth of the Messiah in Bethlehem, 700 years before Christ was born. This once insignificant village has gained eternal prominence. God revealed through Micah these promises: the remnant will remain; He will gather His own from the ends of the earth; and, Zion will be restored.

There has been a great deal of controversy amongst Bible scholars throughout the years as to when Christ was actually born. Many think that December 25, the day we celebrate as His birthday, is incorrect. More likely, His birth was in the spring, because in December shepherds would not have had their flocks out in the open on the hillsides. With December being a fairly cold month in this region, the sheep would have been in caves or other shelters.

The important point here is not the *exact* date when Christ was born, but that *He was born*. And that He was born in the city of Bethlehem, thus fulfilling this prophecy of Micah. This is a fact, authenticated by history.

Micah 5:2-4

"[a]But as for you, Bethlehem Ephrathah, *Too* little to be among the clans of Judah, From you One will go forth for Me to be ruler in Israel. [b]His goings forth are from long ago, From the days of eternity."
3 Therefore He will give them *up* until the time When she who is in labor has borne a child. Then the remainder of His brethren Will return to the sons of Israel. 4 And He will arise and shepherd *His flock* In the strength of the LORD, In the majesty of the name of the LORD His God. And they will [c]remain, Because [d]at that time He will be great
To the ends of the earth.

Notice the opening of the second verse, "But as for you, Bethlehem Ephrathah...." Bethlehem was relatively small, with nothing to distinguish it from many other small communities around Jerusalem. Then God inserted this little conjunction, "But". Things would change in 700 years, when Jesus would be born here. Bethlehem would become a very renowned place.

The Davidic line had regressed to peasants. No longer were any of David's relatives living in the Bethlehem area. They were scattered, so it was highly unlikely that anyone in David's line would be born there.

---

a. Micah 5:2 Ch 5:1 in Heb; b. Or *His appearances are from long ago, from days of old*
c. Micah 5:4 Or *live* in safety; d. Lit *now*

However, there *was* a family in the line of David living in Nazareth, about 90 miles from the village of Bethlehem where the Son of God was to be born. God's master plan was at work here, as the people were directed to return to their original hometown to pay taxes. This required Joseph and Mary to travel from Nazareth to Bethlehem, where Jesus was born. Thus, Caesar Augustus was used by God when he signed the tax bill that moved Mary and Joseph out of Nazareth, to Bethlehem.

"From you One will go forth for Me to be ruler in Israel." This One was coming to do the will of God and to accomplish His plan. He was "From the days of eternity," and "His goings forth are from long ago."

John 1:2-4
[a]He was in the beginning with God. 3 All things came into being through Him, and apart from Him nothing came into being that has come into being. 4 In Him was life, and the life was the Light of men.

Jesus came into the world and put on the clothing of humanity, yet His existence was from everlasting – before His human birth.

In Micah 5:3, the first part of the verse says, "Therefore He will give them *up*." In His First Coming to the earth, Jesus was rejected by the Jewish people. He gave them up and eventually they were dispersed among the nations, scattered by the judgment of God. The Great Tribulation period is the final travail through which the nation must pass. After this, the remnant of the brethren shall return to Israel. The Jewish people will be re-gathered from their worldwide dispersion.

Notice the beginning of Micah 5:4. "And He will arise and shepherd *His flock*." Jesus is the Shepherd

---

a. John 1:2 Lit *This one*

who feeds His flock, the Shepherd to the Church, and also to the nation Israel.

This will occur after His Second Coming and after the seven year Tribulation. Jesus is the One who was born in Bethlehem and who was rejected, yet He will feed His flock. This describes His care, His wonderful care, His protection and His salvation.

He is the Good Shepherd who laid down His life for His sheep (Psalm 22). He is that Great Shepherd who keeps His sheep, even today (Psalm 23). And He is the Chief Shepherd who is coming to be our King of kings and Lord of lords (Psalm 24).

CHAPTER 61: A PURE LANGUAGE

The Book of Zephaniah was written sometime between 640 and 612 BC. A contemporary of Jeremiah, the prophet Zephaniah resided in Jerusalem. It is thought by many Bible scholars that Zephaniah was the great-grandson of the former king of Judah, Hezekiah.

Zephaniah's prophecy concerned both Judah's immediate and long-range judgments from God. He ministered to Judah during the years before the total destruction of the nation, when young Josiah was king. Josiah, most likely influenced by Zephaniah, began as a very good king and instituted sweeping reforms. But even those efforts were not enough, for Judah fell deeper and deeper into apostasy and sin.

Written in Judah and primarily to Judah, the Book of Zephaniah is a message of judgment. The prophet graphically uses the 53 verses of this book to describe the coming wrath to befall Judah, Philistia, Moab, Ammon, Kush, Nineveh, and Assyria.

The sins and coming destruction of Jerusalem is given special emphasis. As always, God gives a hope of future blessings that are available to all of God's people, Jew and Gentile alike, if they will obediently turn to Him.

In Chapter 3, we see the promised remnant of Israel will be restored and there will be worldwide rejoicing.

Observe the themes that this prophet covers. 1) God is not prejudiced. 2) He hates sin and loves obedience, universally. 3) He wants all of us to have pure hearts – not hypocritical outward shows of piety. 4) The coming day of the LORD will bring judgment far greater than anything the world has ever known. 5) Renewed fellowship with God is available to all who have genuinely repentant hearts.

Zephaniah 3:9

"For then I will [a]give to the peoples purified lips, That all of them may call on the name of the LORD, To serve Him [b]shoulder to shoulder.

The narrative of the restoration of Israel begins at the end of Zephaniah.

My first thought was to name this section *A New Language*. To some extent, it is a new language – a pure, clean language. No one will complain about my North Carolina drawl or a New Yorker's northern accent. Occasionally, I've been asked why I talk so slowly. I've responded, "Sometimes you should think about what you say." Perhaps you have heard the old saying, "Say what you think." Perhaps it should be the opposite, "Think what you say." It would help prevent "foot-in-mouth-itis."

At any rate, this pure language will not be shaped by our culture. It will enable us to serve the LORD in harmony. More importantly, a main characteristic of this pure language is there will be no blasphemy or vulgarity. No useless words will be spoken.

---

a. Zephaniah 3:9 Lit *change*; b. Lit *with one shoulder*

CHAPTER 62: A HINGE IN PROPHECY

There are more Messianic prophesies in the Book of Zechariah, written between 520 and 518 B.C., than in any book of the other minor prophets – perhaps as many as in all of them combined. Chapters 1-8 cover about two years during the rebuilding of the temple. The time period is precise because the eighth month of the second year of King Darius, the Mede is referenced. Chapters 9-14, written some years later (around 480 B.C.) cover approximately a ten year period after the temple is completed.

Zechariah's name means "God remembers." He was the son of Berechiah. He and his father were among the exiles who returned to Jerusalem under Zerubbabel. He and Haggai were in Jerusalem at the same time, both exhorting the people to rebuild the temple.

Zechariah's specific Messianic prophesies include the righteous Branch in Chapter 6 (also mentioned in Chapter 3), the triumphal entry on the colt of a donkey in Chapter 9 and, in Chapter 11, the betrayal for 30 pieces of silver. Many other prophecies pertaining to the Millennial Kingdom and the end times are also included.

Zechariah tells the nation that future blessings are dependent upon the people's obedience to God and His Word. The coming of Messiah is central to the book; His power, betrayal and Kingdom. This same Zechariah is mentioned in Matthew.

Matthew 23:35
so that upon you may fall *the guilt* of all the righteous blood shed on earth, from the blood of righteous Abel to the blood of Zechariah, the son of Berechiah, whom you murdered between the [a]temple and the altar.

---

a. Matthew 23:35 Or *sanctuary*

Zechariah was martyred in the temple, or more specifically, between the temple and the altar. The following outline is of the apocalyptic visions of Zechariah, both Messianic and Millennial. (Chapters 1-6.) All of these visions occurred during one night.

1. Riders Under the Myrtle Trees – Zechariah 1:7-17
2. The Four Horns – Zechariah 1:18-19
3. The Four Smiths (Carpenters) – Zechariah 1:20-21
4. Man with a Measuring Line – Zechariah 2
5. Joshua and Satan – Zechariah 3:1-7
6. The Branch – Zechariah 3:8-10
7. The Lampstand and Two Olive Trees – Zechariah 4
8. The Flying Roll or Flying Scroll – Zechariah 5:1-4
9. Woman in the Basket (Ephah) – Zechariah 5:5-11
10. Four Chariots – Zechariah 6

Zechariah 3:8-9

> Now listen, Joshua the high priest, you and your friends who are sitting in front of you—indeed they are men who are a symbol, for behold, I am going to bring in My servant the [a]Branch. 9 For behold, the stone that I have set before Joshua; on one stone are seven eyes. Behold, I will engrave an inscription on it,' declares the Lord of hosts, 'and I will remove the iniquity of that land in one day.

"My servant the Branch" is none other than our Lord and Savior, Jesus Christ. This depiction is found in several other places in the Bible. (See Isaiah 11:1 and Jeremiah 23:5.)

In the Millennial Kingdom, Christ will be our Sovereign King and the Great Shepherd. Note that the Branch is also the Stone – the same Stone seen by Daniel in his vision (Daniel 2:34-35.) It is that Stone, cut out not by human hands, that obliterated the great

---

a. Zechariah 3:8 Lit *Sprout*

image Daniel saw in his dream. There are seven eyes on the Stone. Seven is the number of completeness in the Hebrew numeric system, and those seven eyes indicate that Christ has complete knowledge and wisdom. God will "remove the iniquity of that land in one day," in the future time of the Millennial Kingdom, after the end of the Great Tribulation.

Zechariah 3:10
'In that day,' declares the LORD of hosts, 'every one of you will invite his neighbor to *sit* under *his* vine and under *his* fig tree.'"

The turmoil and trouble we have in our present day is mild compared to what will happen during the years of Tribulation. In "that day" at the end of the Great Tribulation, peace and contentment will prevail.

Zechariah 9:9
Rejoice greatly, O daughter of Zion! Shout *in triumph*, O daughter of Jerusalem! Behold, your king is coming to you; He is [a]just and endowed with salvation, Humble, and mounted on a donkey, Even on a colt, the [b]foal of a donkey.

This verse is among the most well known verses in the Bible. On Palm Sunday, we often hear a sermon on Matthew 21:1-5, with this prophecy of Zechariah repeated. It is a key verse, a hinge on which prophecy turns.

As we read the account in the New Testament, which is commonly referred to as the "Triumphal Entry," we see prophecy precisely fulfilled. Zechariah exhorts us to "Rejoice greatly." The prophecy of Messiah's First Coming was realized as He declared Himself King of kings.

---

a. Zechariah 9:9 Or *vindicated and victorious*; b. Lit *son of a female donkey*

Matthew 21:1-5
The Triumphal Entry

> When they had approached Jerusalem and had come to Bethphage, at the Mount of Olives, then Jesus sent two disciples, 2 saying to them, "Go into the village opposite you, and immediately you will find a donkey tied *there* and a colt with her; untie them and bring them to Me. 3 If anyone says anything to you, you shall say, 'The Lord has need of them,' and immediately he will send them." 4 This [a]took place to fulfill what was spoken through the prophet:
>
> 5 "SAY TO THE DAUGHTER OF ZION,
> 'BEHOLD YOUR KING IS COMING TO YOU,
> GENTLE, AND MOUNTED ON A DONKEY,
> EVEN ON A COLT, THE FOAL OF A BEAST OF BURDEN.'"

Notice there is something different about this particular entry into Jerusalem. Christ had been to Jerusalem many times before, and had always entered in a very low-key, non-obtrusive way, through the Sheep Gate. These verses specifically describe Him as being lowly and riding on a colt, the foal of a donkey. However, this time as He entered He drew attention to Himself. Indeed it was a triumphal entry, which culminated with Christ jubilantly, victoriously and *triumphantly* overcoming all.

At this hinge in prophecy, Christ came to earth and accomplished what He had set out to do. The time had come for Him to fulfill His destiny on this earth, His First Coming. In the next few days He would be beaten, crucified, and would overcome death, paying for the sins of mankind – *past, present, and future.* The Scripture says, "BEHOLD, YOUR KING." He fulfilled His vows and the will of His Father.

---

a. Matthew 21:4 Lit *has happened*

Salvation should be viewed as victory or deliverance. Jesus Christ is the King who came to deliver His people. He took a non-obtrusive approach to this kingship, in that He did not threaten any earthly kingdoms.

To quote Jesus, His "kingdom is not of this world." (John 18:36) His Kingdom that surpasses all other kingdoms is the future world – the Millennium and forevermore.

CHAPTER 63: BETRAYAL OF THE GOOD SHEPHERD

Zechariah 11:12-13

I said to them, "If it is good in your sight, give *me* my wages; but if not, [a]never mind!" So they weighed out thirty *shekels* of silver as my wages. 13 Then the Lord said to me, "Throw it to the potter, *that* magnificent price at which I was valued by them." So I took the thirty *shekels* of silver and threw them to the potter in the house of the LORD.

To put this in context, look forward five and a half centuries, to a night when Judas Iscariot approached the chief priests and fulfilled this prophecy.

Matthew 26:14-15

Then one of the twelve, named Judas Iscariot, went to the chief priests 15 and said, "What are you willing to give me [b]to [c]betray Him to you?" And they weighed out thirty [d]pieces of silver to him.

The price paid for Christ is quite interesting. Even in that day, it was not a great price. The priests were just not willing to pay very much for the life of Jesus. These verses depict the ultimate betrayal.

There have been devastating betrayals throughout history – before, during and after this event. Some have occurred in our own country, such as the selling of secrets to our enemies. A large sum paid to a traitor, perhaps millions of dollars, is still a very low price compared to the value of the lives that can be lost. This paltry sum for our Lord Jesus was offensive – beneath contempt. Matthew adequately describes the betrayer, and verifies prophecy being fulfilled.

a. Zechariah 11:12 Lit *cease*
b. Matthew 26:15 Lit *and I will*; c. Or *deliver*; d. I.e. silver shekels

Matthew 27:3-8

Then when Judas, who had betrayed Him, saw that He had been condemned, he felt remorse and returned the thirty [a]pieces of silver to the chief priests and elders, 4 saying, "I have sinned by betraying innocent blood." But they said, "What is that to us? See *to that* yourself!" 5 And he threw the pieces of silver into the temple sanctuary and departed; and he went away and hanged himself. 6 The chief priests took the pieces of silver and said, "It is not lawful to put them into the temple treasury, since it is the price of blood." 7 And they conferred together and [b]with the money bought the Potter's Field as a burial place for strangers. 8 For this reason that field has been called the Field of Blood to this day.

---

a. Matthew 27:3 Or *silver shekels*
b. Matthew 27:7 Lit *from them*

CHAPTER 64: THE DELIVERANCE OF ISRAEL

In the End Times, near the end of Tribulation, the world will be against Israel. At that time God will protect them, as this next verse explains.

Zechariah 12:10
"I will pour out on the house of David and on the inhabitants of Jerusalem, [a]the Spirit of grace and of supplication, so that they will look on Me whom they have pierced; and they will mourn for Him, as one mourns for an only son, and they will weep bitterly over Him like the bitter weeping over a firstborn.

Many people believe that the Jewish people returning to that land since 1948, when the nation of Israel was restored, fulfilled prophecy. However, there is certainly not a "Spirit of grace and of supplication," which negates this belief. This prophecy will be fulfilled when God removes the iniquity (sin) from that land. Undeniably, that has not yet happened.

Revelation 1:7
BEHOLD, HE IS COMING WITH THE CLOUDS, and every eye will see Him, even those who pierced Him; and all the tribes of the earth will mourn over Him. So it is to be. Amen.

At this time, most of the Jewish people do not believe Jesus Christ was the Messiah. When He returns, "every eye will see Him" – even those who pierced Him. They will be very aware of who He was when He came the first time, when they failed to recognize Him. John describes exactly what will take place when Jesus returns.

---

a. Zechariah 12:10 Or *a spirit*

There will be great mourning in the world, because He will be recognized as the one they crucified, their Savior, the One who died for their sins.

John 1:9-11
There was the true Light [a]which, coming into the world, enlightens every man. 10 He was in the world, and the world was made through Him, and the world did not know Him. 11 He came to His [b]own, and those who were His own did not receive Him.

Zechariah 13:1
"In that day a fountain will be opened for the house of David and for the inhabitants of Jerusalem, for sin and for impurity.

Ezekiel 36:25-26
Then I will sprinkle clean water on you, and you will be clean; I will cleanse you from all your filthiness and from all your idols. 26 Moreover, I will give you a new heart and put a new spirit within you; and I will remove the heart of stone from your flesh and give you a heart of flesh.

Revelation 22:1
Then he showed me a river of the water of life, [c]clear as crystal, coming from the throne of God and of [d]the Lamb,

All of these events will take place after the Tribulation, when the Lord returns. He will purge the iniquity of that land, and of the entire world (what's left of it) in one day. Thus, the restoration and cleansing of Israel, and of all believers in the world, will be accomplished.

---

a. John 1:9 Or *which enlightens every person coming into the world*
b. John 1:11 Or *own things, possessions, domain*
c. Revelation 22:1 Lit *bright*; d. Or *the Lamb. In the middle of its street, and on either side of the river, was*

CHAPTER 65: RETURN OF THE MESSIAH

In our review of the Book of Zechariah, we have discovered that it is, without a doubt, an apocalyptic book. Now we come to the ultimate conclusion of adversity in the Bible.

Zechariah 14:1-2

Behold, a day is coming for the Lord when the spoil taken from you will be divided among you. 2 For I will gather all the nations against Jerusalem to battle, and the city will be captured, the houses plundered, the women ravished and half of the city exiled, but the rest of the people will not be cut off from the city.

This might make an excellent headline for newspapers, if they are still in existence at the end of the Tribulation. The "day of the LORD" is no longer coming – it has arrived – in this prophecy. All of the nations have been gathered against Jerusalem to do battle – a battle they will not win. It will appear they are winning when the first half of the city is taken and all these atrocious events take place; however, the last of the second verse reveals that the remnant of the people "will not be cut off from the city."

As this is being written, the United Nations has moved their Peacekeepers into Lebanon to prevent Israel's enemies from firing rockets and causing more upheaval in that land. Recent history indicates that other nations are becoming, with the exception of the United States, more and more reluctant to offer Israel assistance. Perhaps the majority feels that Israel is the problem; however, God's Word reveals this assumption is false.

Genesis 12:3

And I will bless those who bless you, And the one who [a]curses you I will [b]curse. And in you all the families of the earth will be blessed."

Zechariah 14:3

Then the LORD will go forth and fight against those nations, as [c]when He fights on a day of battle.

There is no doubt – the King of kings, the Lord of lords – is going to win this battle. Help will not come from the United States, or from Great Britain, or even from the United Nations. It will not come from the north, south, east, or west. Help will come from above – from that undefeatable Person, the Deliverer.

Zechariah 14:4-5

In that day His feet will stand on the Mount of Olives, which is in front of Jerusalem on the east; and the Mount of Olives will be split in its middle from east to west by a very large valley, so that half of the mountain will move toward the north and the other half toward the south. 5 You will flee by the valley of My mountains, for the valley of the mountains will reach to Azel; yes, you will flee just as you fled before the earthquake in the days of Uzziah king of Judah. Then the LORD, my God, will come, *and* all the holy ones with [d]Him!

When Jesus ascended back to Heaven after His First Coming, His disciples were told that He would return in a like manner.

---

a. Genesis 12:3 Or *reviles*; b. Or *bind under a curse*
c. Zechariah 14:3 Lit *His day of fighting*
d. Zechariah 14:5 So the versions; Heb *You*

Acts 1:11
> They also said, "Men of Galilee, why do you stand
> looking into [a]the sky? This Jesus, who has been taken up
> from you into heaven, will come in just the same way as
> you have watched Him go into heaven."

His feet will touch down on the Mount of Olives.
"You will flee by the valley of My mountains" is
intended by the LORD as an escape route from the
devastation He is about to wreak upon the earth.
Continuing in Zechariah 14:5, we see that Jesus and
all the saints will join those left in Jerusalem. And in
Revelation 19:14 we see that the armies of Heaven will
follow.

Revelation 19:14
> And the armies which are in heaven, clothed in fine linen,
> white and clean, were following Him on white horses.

Zechariah 14:8
> And in that day living waters will flow out of Jerusalem,
> half of them toward the eastern sea and the other half
> toward the western sea; it will be in summer as well as
> in winter.

The river of life that flows from the throne of God
and of the Lamb (Christ) is the life-giving stream
mentioned in Ezekiel 47:1-12 and in Revelation 22:1-6.
The eastern sea is the Dead Sea, and the western sea the
Mediterranean, as can be seen on a map of Jerusalem.

Zechariah 14:9
God Will Be King Over All

> And the LORD will be king over all the earth; in that day
> the LORD will be *the only* one, and His name *the only*
> one.

a. Acts 1:11 Or *heaven*

This will be the day of the LORD, the fulfillment of the prophecy of His Second Coming, when He will assume the Lordship of the remaining world. This is the Shepherd who in Psalm 22 died for His sheep; our leader in Psalm 23 who caused us to lie down beside the still waters, led us in paths of righteousness, and led us through the valley of the shadow; and now, as in Psalm 24, has returned as our sovereign King.

Zechariah 14:10-11

All the land will be changed into a plain from Geba to Rimmon south of Jerusalem; but [a]Jerusalem will rise and remain on its site from Benjamin's Gate as far as the place of the First Gate to the Corner Gate, and from the Tower of Hananel to the king's wine presses. 11 [b]People will live in it, and there will no longer be a curse, for Jerusalem will dwell in security.

This is the grand finale. Jerusalem will be raised up and inhabited. It will be restored beyond its former glory, more beautiful than ever before. It will be a fertile land, the land of milk and honey, as it was when God took His people into the promised land.

The rugged terrain will be smoothed over. Certainly if the LORD can split the mountain asunder He can level out this rugged land and make it a fertile plain.

In the land today there is war and destruction, terrorism, and all kinds of evil. For the first time in history this will be a peaceful land, instead of a land of turmoil and war. When Jerusalem is restored, there will be a distinct difference from what has occurred down through the ages.

---

a. Zechariah 14:10 Lit *it*
b. Zechariah 14:11 Lit *They*

CHAPTER 66: PUNISHMENT OF NATIONS THAT FOUGHT AGAINST ISRAEL

Zechariah 14:12-13

Now this will be the plague with which the LORD will strike all the peoples who have gone to war against Jerusalem; their flesh will rot while they stand on their feet, and their eyes will rot in their sockets, and their tongue will rot in their mouth. 13 It will come about in that day that a great panic from the LORD will [a]fall on them; and they will seize one another's hand, and the hand of one will [b]be lifted against the hand of another.

A tremendous heat would be required to dissolve flesh, eyes, and tongues. Whatever means the LORD uses, it will be horrific. It is very distressing to contemplate. Nonetheless, in His righteous anger, the LORD will mete out this punishment. Doubtless, there will be much confusion in the army that battles Jerusalem. They will turn against each other in this final battle.

Zechariah 14:14

Judah also will fight at Jerusalem; and the wealth of all the surrounding nations will be gathered, gold and silver and garments in great abundance.

Currently, Israel is a country that is dependant on others for their well-being, their protection, and their livelihood. When this great battle ends, Israel will have wealth (gold, silver and apparel) in great abundance, garnered from the people who fought against them. Christ will take control, and Israel will be the commercial center of the world.

---

a. Zechariah 14:13 Lit *be among*; b. Lit *rise up against*

Zechariah 14:16-17

> Then it will come about that any who are left of all the nations that went against Jerusalem will go up from year to year to worship the King, the LORD of hosts, and to celebrate the Feast of Booths. 17 And it will be that whichever of the families of the earth does not go up to Jerusalem to worship the King, the LORD of hosts, there will be no rain on them.

Not everyone will agree with the leadership of these nations. Some will not approve of turning against Israel. If our country ever reaches the point of fighting against Israel, I believe a large portion of our population will be absolutely against that decision.

These verses indicate that not only the remnant of Israel will be saved, but also some out of each nation of the Gentiles will enter the Kingdom. People from all the nations are to go to Jerusalem to worship the LORD and to celebrate the Feast of Booths (Tabernacles). This will be a requirement for all people.

During the Millennium, this will be a time of testing for those of the great multitude who remain after the Tribulation. If any do not go and worship, rain will be withheld from them.

Throughout the Bible, recorded events indicate droughts were sent by God as punishments. One of the longest (the foreseen seven-year drought) occurred during the time Joseph was in Egypt. In other examples, rain was withheld for specific periods of time. In all cases, the LORD was at work. A land that is prosperous and green can be turned into a desert, temporarily or permanently. This is one of the ways God judges people and lands. Unmistakably, He will use this as a disciplinary tool during the Millennium.

CHAPTER 67: THE DESIRE OF ALL NATIONS

Haggai was written in 520 BC, in less than four months. Because of the details given, the specific time-frame can be identified, down to the month. Not many prophecies were dated this closely. Quite a period of time – about 14 years – had elapsed since Zerubbabel, (the governor of Judah) and Joshua (the high priest) led the first return of exiles to Jerusalem with the mission of rebuilding the temple of God.

This group of exiles included Haggai, who was advanced in age. The group, who had great aspirations, had run into hard times. They had allowed opposition, worldly influences, and the scarcity of resources to discourage them – even to the point of quitting after rebuilding only the temple foundation.

The Jews' neglect in finishing this job was made worse by their preoccupation with constructing elaborate homes for themselves. The Spirit of the LORD came to the prophet Haggai, prompting him to stir the people to resume building the temple. The best way possible for him to accomplish this was to remind them of what they had lost, and the blessings that would come to those who put God first in their lives.

Haggai's message was simple. In order for a project to be completed, it first must be started. Although the construction had begun, it had not really gotten off the ground. A job half-done is a job not done.

It is important to avoid compromising situations that allow other things to override what we should do for the LORD. Sometimes we settle for "good enough" when we could have the best. Our standards of success hold no lasting contentment when we place our concerns ahead of those of God.

Haggai 1:5-8

Now therefore, thus says the LORD of hosts, "[a]Consider your ways! 6 You have sown much, but [b]harvest little; *you* eat, but *there is* not *enough* to be satisfied; *you* drink, but *there is* [c]not *enough* to become drunk; *you* put on clothing, but no one is warm *enough*; and he who earns, earns wages *to put* into a purse with holes."

7 Thus says the LORD of hosts, "[d]Consider your ways! 8 Go up to the [e]mountains, bring wood and rebuild the [f]temple, that I may be pleased with it and be glorified," says the LORD.

In this passage, the LORD exhorted the people to consider what they were doing. The LORD said this twice! (When He says something once it is very important, but when He says something twice it is very, *very* important.) He reminded the people of something difficult to do – to look objectively at themselves. Sometimes we have difficulty "seeing the forest for the trees." Our vision becomes obscured by the things we want and attempt to acquire by our own power.

God pointed out that the people had been ignoring Him – at their own expense – for they had not been blessed. With limited resources, they barely had enough to exist. Had they been following God's will, their cup would have been running over with plentiful blessings.

As in so many of God's messages to His people through His prophets, a simple three-step solution was given. They were to: 1) go up to the mountain, 2) bring wood, and 3) build a house.

Acquiring the wood and building this temple was not without much labor and effort, especially with the

---

a. Haggai 1:5 Lit *Set your heart on*
b. Haggai 1:6 Lit *bring in*; c. Lit *not becoming drunk*
d. Haggai 1:7 Lit *Set your heart on*
e. Haggai 1:8 Lit *mountain*; f. Lit *house*

tools available at that time. But when God wants you to do something, you must be willing to do whatever it might require.

Haggai 2:6-7
For thus says the LORD of hosts, 'Once more [a]in a little while, I am going to shake the heavens and the earth, the sea also and the dry land. 7 I will shake all the nations; and [b]they will come with the wealth of all nations, and I will fill this house with glory,' says the LORD of hosts.

God's instructions, through Haggai, reminded His people to concentrate on important things rather than the worldly. "I am going to shake the heavens and the earth, the sea also and the dry land," tells of His future judgment during the Great Tribulation.

"This house" was not the temple under construction; rather, it referred to a series of houses or temples. The first was Solomon's opulent temple. Zerubbabel's temple was later demolished by Herod. Herod's temple (never finished) was built on a grand scale. Into Herod's temple came the glory of Christ, in human flesh. Herod's temple was destroyed by Titus in AD 70.

Now on that site is the Mosque of Omar, one of the most holy shrines in the world of Islam. The Great Tribulation temple will be built on this very site, and after that the Millennial Temple. The grandness and beauty of this final temple will far surpass any of the temples built in the past.

Haggai 2:9
'The latter glory of this house will be greater than the former,' says the LORD of hosts, 'and in this place I will give peace,' declares the LORD of hosts."

---

a. Haggai 2:6 Lit *it is a little*
b. Haggai 2:7 Or *the desire of all nations will come*

At the very time I am writing this there is unrest throughout the world, especially in and around Israel, where this temple will be built. Wars are constantly being fought. Israel is encompassed by enemies. Peace is certainly not likely to occur without divine intervention. The Lord Jesus Christ will accomplish what the United Nations, the United States, and all the other entities of the world have failed to do.

When Jesus was on earth the first time, He went to Herod's temple. This last temple will be the most grand, its glory beyond description. When Christ sets foot in this final temple, there will be peace in the world. The peace described in this verse is a different kind of peace.

Jesus came to earth to accomplish many things, chief of which to bring us His grace and salvation. In so doing, He brought a great peace to our souls – the peace we have in knowing we are safe in Him.

Philippians 4:7
> And the peace of God, which surpasses all [a]comprehension, will guard your hearts and your minds in Christ Jesus.

You, too, can have this marvelous peace "which surpasses all comprehension." It is a gift that you need only accept. Nothing else is required.

Romans 10:9
> [b]that if you confess with your mouth Jesus as Lord, and believe in your heart that God raised Him from the dead, you will be saved;

Just believe!

---

a. Philippians 4:7 Lit *mind*
b. Romans 10:9 Or *because*

ABOUT THE AUTHOR

David *(Dave)* Hobson, the son of a sharecropper, was born in the foothills of North Carolina. When he was eight years old his family moved to the Greensboro area, where he has remained. The oldest of seven children, Dave worked on tobacco farms until he reached adulthood.

As a young adult, Dave became a private pilot and enjoyed hundreds of hours in the air. He was known for giving his passengers a flight they would not soon forget. Also an avid water skier, Dave spent thousands of hours on the beautiful lakes of North Carolina and Virginia.

He served three years in the National Guard, followed by three years in the U.S. Army as a paratrooper in the 82nd Airborne Division. Dave loved "jumping" and continued as a civilian for some time. Upon his honorable discharge from the Army, he began a long and successful career with Duke Power (now Duke Energy). After an early "golden parachute" retirement from the utility, he worked a variety of odd jobs, just to keep busy and to help his friends. It was during a long drive for one of these jobs that he found and began regularly listening to a Christian radio station.

Hearing the teachings of Dr. J. Vernon McGee, Dr. David Jeremiah and others on the radio led Dave to rededicate his life to Christ and get involved in a local church body. He served as a Senior Adult Sunday School teacher for several years, of which he said that (in preparing for the lessons) he "learned far more than those in the class." Dave also served as a deacon, sang in the choir, and helped maintain the church buildings and grounds as long as he was able.

About 15 years ago, Dave began a personal in-depth study of God's Word. From this study, *The Scarlet Thread: Finding Jesus through Old Testament Prophecy* was born. Dave's prayer is for this book to bless and encourage all who read it.

In the course of his career with Duke Power Company, Dave met his wife of 40 years, Linda. The couple has two sons, five grandchildren and three great-grandsons, who all reside in North Carolina.

Made in the USA
Columbia, SC
20 June 2025

59545425R00150